A CUP OF COMFORT®
Book of
Christmas Prayer

Prayers AND *Stories* THAT BRING YOU
CLOSER TO *God* DURING THE *Holiday*

EDITED BY SUSAN B. TOWNSEND

adamsmedia
Avon, Massachusetts

Dedicated to the memory of my father,
Robert David Armstrong

(1923–2008).

A *Cup of Comfort*® is a registered trademark of F+W Media, Inc.

Published by
Adams Media, a division of F+W Media, Inc.
57 Littlefield Street, Avon, MA 02322 U.S.A.
www.adamsmedia.com and *www.cupofcomfort.com*

ISBN 13: 978-1-4405-0051-0
ISBN 10: 1-4405-0051-7
Printed in the United States of America.

J I H G F E D C B

Library of Congress Cataloging-in-Publication Data
is available from the publisher.

This publication is designed to provide accurate and authoritative information with regard to the subject matter covered. It is sold with the understanding that the publisher is not engaged in rendering legal, accounting,
or other professional advice. If legal advice or other expert assistance is
required, the services of a competent professional person should be sought.

—From a *Declaration of Principles* jointly adopted by a Committee of
the American Bar Association and a Committee of Publishers and
Associations

Many of the designations used by manufacturers and sellers to distinguish their products are claimed as trademarks. Where those designations appear in this book and Adams Media was aware of a trademark
claim, the designations have been printed with initial capital letters.

Unless otherwise noted, the Bible used as a source is *Holy Bible: New
Living Translation*, Tyndale House Publishers.

This book is available at quantity discounts for bulk purchases.
For information, please call 1-800-289-0963.

CONTENTS

CONTENTS

Contents

Acknowledgments

My deepest gratitude goes to Paula Munier, the Director of Acquisitions and Innovation at Adams Media. Her talent, wisdom, and support as my editor made this book possible. I'd also like to thank Matthew Glazer, Brendan O'Neill, and the other terrific people at Adams for their skill, hard work, and endless patience.

INTRODUCTION

"If my hands are fully occupied in holding on to something, I can neither give nor receive."

—Dorothee Sölle

Unless you live in a cave on a deserted island, no one needs to tell you Christmas is coming. Mail-order catalogs arrive in late September, and within days after Thanksgiving, the store shelves are stocked with every imaginable Christmas item.

Your calendar begins to fill up with astonishing and often terrifying speed as parties, pageants, and shopping expeditions are penciled in. Your list of things to do turns into a novel, and you find yourself longing for January. Even the simple act of attending church is transformed into a production as the most well-intentioned believers get caught up in the worldly obligations of the season.

Most people would agree it's a far cry from the night a baby was born under a star in a stable in Bethlehem. This was no ordinary infant, but God Incarnate, and the only people in attendance were his parents and a few shepherds. There was no media circus or magazines bidding millions of dollars for first photos of the child. Few people were aware that the newborn cries heard that miraculous night came from the Messiah promised by God for thousands of years.

As you make your way through this holiday season, allow the stories, devotionals, prayers, and scripture in this book to help you escape some of the commercialism and create a more Christ-centered Christmas. It is our hope that you will be inspired and encouraged to view Christmas as more than just one day when we open gifts, eat a sumptuous feast, and worship the Lord.

Generous and gifted contributors will introduce you to "Advent"—the weeks leading up to Christmas; "The Twelve Days of Christmas" following the celebration on December 25; and finally, "Epiphany," the day that commemorates the Magi's visit to the Christ child. Their experiences will reassure you that you're not alone in your struggle to glorify God and focus on the true purpose of the season. Their words will make you smile, reminisce, and perhaps even cry, but most importantly, they will remind you of the most awesome gift in the history of the world.

—*Susan B. Townsend*

PART ONE

ADVENT:

DECEMBER 1 — DECEMBER 24

INTRODUCTION

Counting down the days for something special can be difficult, but most of us would agree there are things well worth waiting for. In some respects, the waiting often prepares us for the event to come. Whether it's the birth of a child or a move to a new city, the days and weeks beforehand allow us to absorb the reality of a significant change in our lives. Our days are often occupied with joyful anticipation, and even when we're not physically involved in preparing for the big day, our minds and hearts are filled with eager anticipation.

In the same way, we should rejoice at the prospect of welcoming our Lord on Christmas Day, and the days leading up to his birth should be filled with ardent and enthusiastic expectation. Many believers celebrate the coming of their Messiah during a period known as Advent, which traditionally consists of the four Sundays leading up to Christmas Day.

During this period, believers prepare for Christ's coming in a variety of ways. Worship and scripture readings during this time acknowledge both Christ's first coming as prophesied in the Old Testament and His eventual second coming as described in the New Testament. A popular tradition often incorporated into the Advent season is a circular wreath symbolizing God's eternal love and consisting of four candles with one candle in the center. The wreath's greenery stands for Christ's promise of everlasting life, and each candle represents an important aspect of His life. A candle is lit on each Sunday with the one in the center lit on Christmas Eve. The growing brightness is a reminder that the birth of our Savior—the "Light of the World"—is close at hand.

As with any long-anticipated event, Advent involves both physical and emotional preparation. Most of us are familiar with the endless to-do list involved with getting ready for Christmas, but without the time it takes to develop a true sense of spiritual readiness, the real message of the season may be lost.

So, slow down, take a deep breath, and enter the blessed weeks before Christmas with your heart and mind open to the miraculous day when God became man. Welcome the Lord into your home to help you prepare for a birthday party fit for a King.

December 1
Advent at Hall House

I live in the sunny south, so I've rarely experienced those cold temperatures that usher in the Christmas season for so many others. I've never enjoyed shopping much, so I don't start Christmas searching for sales and discounts and coming home with my arms laden with packages. At my house, Christmas officially starts when I yell for my youngest son, "Bring up the box marked 'Advent Wreath'!"

Most Christians think of the Advent wreath as a cherished spiritual tradition of prayers, candles, and greenery. Perhaps, when they picture the wreath, they see a loving family, gathered around the warm glow of the deep purple tapers rising majestically from the ring of holly. Maybe they get a warm feeling inside, recalling all the prayers recited and sent heavenward. Of course, that would be the Advent wreath tradition over at the perfect house. At the Hall house, the Advent wreath tradition is a little less than perfect.

I introduced my husband to the Advent wreath in the early days of our marriage. He accompanied me to church where the candles were lit and the priest said a special prayer on the four Sundays leading up to Christmas Eve. Growing up in a Catholic home, there had always been an Advent wreath in the house, and when our first Christmas together arrived, my husband and I had a little Advent wreath of our own. For a brief, shining moment we shared something close to a prayerful, meaningful Advent wreath tradition. Then, we had a little boy.

Joey was born on December 28, and by his first Advent, he was hitting his stride in the rambunctious toddler stage. So, the first step in celebrating/childproofing our Advent wreath tradition was our purchase of a *very* sturdy wreath. Our wreath may not have won any decorating awards, but it still stands today like the Rock of Gibraltar. This can be a particularly good thing when a toddler, a dog, or even teenagers are in the proximity of a fire-bearing object.

Keeping the prayers short and sweet seemed like a very good idea, too. So, we bowed our heads for a Bible verse and squeezed in a quick "Come, Lord Jesus, as soon as possible! Amen!"

With the arrival of our daughter, our Advent wreath tradition changed once more. Laney was quiet and serious. She watched everything with her thumb firmly entrenched in her mouth. Joey, on the other hand, was a chatterbox. That child could talk paper off a wall. It seemed perfectly reasonable, at least to me, to invite Joey to add something personal and spiritual to our evening Advent celebration. It was time, I decided, for Joey to participate in the prayer department. Okay, it was really about talking Joey into sharing the all-important fire responsibilities.

We began our prayers with reading short—the shorter the better—passages from the New Testament. Our ultimate goal was to end up on the chapter of the birth of Christ on Christmas Eve. I thought it was a wonderful idea, just like something out of a Norman Rockwell Advent. We'd end our short reading with a little prayer, courtesy of Joey. Another terrific idea, except for the fact that our son wasn't happy with his ten seconds of prayer fame. He desperately wanted to take part in the Bible reading, but he didn't know how to read a word.

Still, I'm not one to discourage my children's growth in the faith. So, that year, as we gathered around the Advent wreath, I would read a short verse and then hand my son the Bible. The stories he told weren't in any Bible I'd ever read, but what he lacked in authenticity, he more than made up for in length. We endured endless, convoluted stories of Jesus and Ninja Turtles charging down Sesame Street in Bethlehem or his preschool playground.

Just when we thought it was time for our "Come, Lord Jesus, Amen," Joey would take a big breath and start up again. Candle wax flowed over the Rock of Gibraltar wreath onto the placemat. Laney fell asleep in my numb arms. Dad's patience wore dangerously thin. I think the most common prayer offered that Advent was one of thanksgiving when Joey finally ran out of words.

Our third and last child came along to join in the tradition, and by then, our family had the whole Advent wreath ritual down to something of an art. We carefully included baby John in the candle-lighting rotation, and during a moment of wisdom, we switched from Bible readings to an Advent booklet. When John was school age, I had a brainstorm. We'd include prayers for special intentions! We figured that would be a wonderful way to involve the kids. The children certainly got involved, but not in the way we had imagined.

Invariably, one of the younger children would have a special intention that Joey decided wasn't "prayer worthy." He didn't think it was right to pray for an "A" on a test or to ask God for help in beating another sports team. He especially didn't think we should bother the Lord with dog prayers.

"Dear Lord, please let Sally quit barking so the neighbors won't complain anymore."

"You can't pray for that!" he shouted.

"Can, too," John replied, just a little louder.

Joey remained adamant and decided that shouting was the best way to prove his point. "You have to pray for people!" The arguing intensified, feelings got hurt, Dad yelled, and tears were shed—all in the glow of our Advent wreath. Eventually, we made it to our "Come, Lord Jesus. Amen!" prayer. I have a feeling that God even heard our Sally dog prayers since she's still here and barking happily.

Our children were here, too, though not always for the first days of Advent. Our youngest child, John was still at home, and he brought the wreath box upstairs. I unpacked the wax-covered Advent wreath and placed the candles in the holders.

Three of the Halls came together to pray and soon enough, twenty-something Halls arrived home for the holidays.

The entire family gatherd again to pray and wait for the Lord's coming. We had taken turns lighting the candles as we remembered the Light of the World. We opened the Bible and reflected while we listened to His word. Finally, we offered our special intentions, trusting in His power to answer our prayers.

As always, there were moments of laughter, joy, tears, and thanksgiving around our dilapidated wreath. There was bound to be an evening when candle wax overflowed and ruined yet another placemat, but that's okay. It's our less-than-perfect Advent tradition, and the Halls wouldn't start the Christmas season any other way.

—*Cathy C. Hall*

Watering the Poinsettias

Do you have the gift of helping others? Do it with all the strength and energy that God supplies. Then everything you do will bring glory to God through Jesus Christ. All glory and power to him forever and ever! Amen.

1 PETER 4:11

The poinsettias were banked three tiers deep around the huge platform in a breathtaking array. The harmony of the choir and the music of the orchestra, as they presented "Go Tell It on the Mountain," swelled around these radiant red blooms. What a glorious beginning to the Advent season.

Now, I found myself dreading every Sunday and every Wednesday because I had to water the poinsettias. I had volunteered before I realized there would be over one hundred plants, all arranged so it was impossible to get to each of them or tell if all of them had been watered. I had to carry water all the way from the custodian's storage room which was always locked.

Long before everyone showed up on Sunday, I found myself grudgingly watering the poinsettias: trying to make sure I didn't miss any, trying to make sure I gave each one enough water, trying not to spill water on the carpet, and trying to finish before people began to assemble.

The second Wednesday, a lady whom I'd never met, came up to me and said abruptly, "I'm the one who bought all the poinsettias. Would you please give those two wilted ones an extra drink of water?" I wanted to say that buying them was easier than watering them, but I didn't.

Another lady approached me with a smile on her face and pointed out one of the largest poinsettias. "That one is mine in memory of my mother." I was grateful it wasn't one of the wilted ones.

"In memory of my mother," went to my heart and began to change my attitude. I remembered all the times I'd bought a poinsettia and placed it in the church in memory of my mother. Watering it was an act of love, not a bothersome chore.

Then, I remembered why the poinsettia is one of the symbols of Christmas. One Christmas Eve in Mexico, a poor little girl gathered weeds on her way to church because she had no gift to give the baby Jesus. The legend has been told that the weeds blossomed into brilliant red flowers. The least I could do was joyfully water these beautiful living symbols of love.

Gifts of love are the most valuable.

—*Jeanette MacMillan*

$\mathcal{D}ecember$ 2
A Star Is Born

$\mathcal{T}$hey weren't the most promising group of actors in the world, but the festive season was fast approaching, and we were aware that many of our young charges in an inner-city children's club had never acted out the true story of Christmas. The leader suggested we make the props, rehearse the pageant, and invite the parents to the gala presentation.

On rehearsal night, I found myself in a tiny room of the church basement surrounded by a mountain of old bath towels, tangled neckties, and oversized housecoats. Reports of our magnificent production had apparently infiltrated the entire neighborhood because unfamiliar little faces began appearing in the dressing room, all pleading for last-minute parts in the performance. Hard pressed to distinguish between stars and stand-ins, I asked a curly headed young fellow who he was supposed to be.

"I'm a character!" he snapped back, and his subsequent behavior proved him quite right. He was not alone. Aggressive shepherds challenged each other with their crooks, and one of the Wise Men tried to stab his peers with a stray safety pin.

I kept reassuring myself that should all other aspects of the production fail to earn top ratings, local drama critics would no doubt be impressed on at least one count. An ingenious church usher had rigged up a wire-and-pulley system to transport the glorious star across the darkened sanctuary and bring it to rest over the manger scene in a grand finale to the pageant. As I was about to discover, however, the Deity has a definite edge on mortals when it comes to astronomy.

The night of the production, in front of a packed house, the organist began to play softly, "O Little Town of Bethlehem." Lights dimmed, and the narrator began to read. Temporarily forgetting her delicate condition, Mary bounded up the stairs to the stage two at a time, only to be restrained by Joseph's loud admonition, "Slow down, stupid, and wait for me."

The innkeeper banged the door in the couple's face, and they retreated to the stable, amid a great deal of crowing and mooing and bleating from the "livestock" backstage.

The spotlight shifted to the ragged shepherds, keeping watch over their cardboard sheep by night. Suddenly, a troop of angels with halos askew stormed the scene, tripping over bed sheet robes and bumping wings as they jostled for the limelight. The shepherds thundered across the stage to the manger scene, most of them forgetting to gaze in adoration at the infant Jesus and choosing instead to peer out into the darkened sanctuary and wave at their parents.

Our redeeming hope lay in the visit of the magi, and there they were, coming up the aisle from the back of the church, complete with every bit of the composure and dignity traditionally associated with such men of rank. High overhead, the splendid tinfoil star was starting its long journey across the sanctuary. "Star of wonder, star of night..."

The scratchy recording of "We Three Kings" was not enhanced by the "squeak, squawk, squeak" of the makeshift clothesline pulley that inched the star along its orbit, a tad jerky, but nevertheless "westward leading, still proceeding." The Wise Men followed suit, their eyes glued to their guiding light.

Suddenly the star came to a premature standstill. Instead of going all the way to its appointed place over the stage, it stopped short and began swaying back and forth in one place as if attacked by opposing forces of magnetism. Intrigued by the unexpected turn of events, the wise ones craned their necks this way and that to better observe the strange phenomenon. Then, they ceased their journey altogether. Instead, they decided to turn around in the middle of the aisle and stare up at their guiding light that had ground to a sudden halt so mysteriously.

The amateur lighting man tried swinging his spotlight along the star's orbit, finally focusing on the source of the problem. A crude splice in the clothesline had refused to negotiate the pulley at the back of the church. The spotlight revealed an embarrassed young usher teetering high up on a rickety stepladder, desperately trying to coax the reluctant star toward its destination with one hand, while waving the magi on with the other.

Wanting to oblige, but determined not to take their eyes off the star, the Wise Men compromised by walking backward down the aisle. Clutching their gold, frankincense, and myrrh, they tried to steady their cardboard crowns while tripping repeatedly over the tails of their bathrobes.

It was an arduous journey without benefit of starlight, but eventually they bumped into the foot of the stage and turned around to face the manger scene.

At this point, Joseph, undaunted by dealing with men of superior station and intellect, instructed them to, "Use the steps, stupid, and make it fast!"

Peering over their shoulders one last time at the star, the Wise Men plodded reluctantly up the steps to present their gifts. An awkward shepherd placed a bent lamb at the foot of the manger, and angels adjusted precarious halos. Joseph and Mary gazed down at their little off-spring with appropriate awe as the organ began to play "Silent Night." An almost holy hush descended upon the scene.

Abruptly, a rapid series of squeaks and squawks intruded upon the sacred moment. As if to make up for lost time, the natal star careened across the sanctuary and swung to a magnificent stop right over the baby. There, it hung by one point, its brilliant tin foil reflecting the spotlight and all but blinding those who gazed too steadily upon its glory.

The Bible tells us that when the Wise Men "saw the star, they rejoiced with exceedingly great joy." In our case, they jumped up and down, pointing and shouting, "Hoo-ray!"

I don't know if it was relief or rapture that brought the audience to their feet, whistling and clapping. They lav-ished such ongoing praise on the entire cast that the light-ing man felt compelled to focus the spotlight on the young usher atop his rickety ladder at the back of the church. He responded by taking a self-conscious bow.

Curiously, there was nothing irreverent about the moment. If anything, it served to reinforce the fact that the greatest tribute of all belongs to God—the one behind the scenes of our life who redeems our inadequate endeavors. Although, at times, God may seem slow, we can rest assured that He is never late.

—Alma Barkman

A Lesson in Planning

So when Mary and Joseph came to present the baby Jesus
to the Lord as the law required, Simeon was there. He took
the child in his arms and praised God, saying, "Sovereign
Lord, now let your servant die in peace, as you have
promised. I have seen your salvation, which you have
prepared for all people."
LUKE 2:27–31

My friend, who is a teacher, is one of those organized plan-
ners who start their Christmas shopping the January after
Christmas. Less than a week after New Year's Day, I found
her packing up a box of Christmas craft kits she had just
ordered online. While I was still contemplating my New
Year's goal of becoming more organized, she was busy planning Christmas art projects for her students next year. If
extreme planning was an Olympic sport, she would have a
shelf full of gold medals.

As for me, I would win the gold for extreme procrastination. Every year, I vow to start my shopping by November
and every year, I'm shopping a week before Christmas. One
Christmas Eve, my ridiculous procrastination had me scur-
rying around the mall like a mouse searching for cheese.
When I finally returned home, I was so stressed I dipped
my hand in one of the Christmas stockings searching for

chocolate. Worse still, I cheated myself out of the joy and peace that Christmas has to offer.

Simeon of the New Testament was a planner. A devout and righteous Jewish man, "he eagerly expected the Messiah to come and rescue Israel." (Luke 2:26) The Holy Spirit had reassured him he would see the Messiah before he died. Simeon had been planning for years for that day to come. When it finally did, he was so ready he instantly recognized Jesus for who He was—the gift of a Savior sent by God to rescue the world.

If we take the time to plan, we'll be able to enjoy the gift of God's perfect plan: Jesus.

—*Jamie Birr*

December 3
A Holy Night in Jail

*I*t wasn't beginning to look like Christmas, or any other holiday, inside the county jail. Trustees still wore their orange jump suits as they pushed breakfast carts into the pods. The inmates still wore their green pants and orange smocks, and the security officers still thumbed through my Bible to see what was in there.

Outside, the weather told a different story. The snow had begun to fall about six-thirty that morning—a rare treat for the Portland, Oregon, area. In pod two at the jail, the women's pod, the ladies couldn't see the snow, but they knew it was cold. My husband had agreed to miss church in order to take me over to the jail in his four-wheel-drive truck. "I'll go get some breakfast," he said. "Call me when you're done."

He dropped me off in front of the jail, but even so, I was covered with snow by the time I made it in the front door. Good thing I wore a turtleneck under my blue chaplain shirt. It was chilly in there. I met up with Vergene, one of the ministry leaders, and we went through the various layers of security. As we trudged down the long hallway of the jail, "the spine," I remembered my first visit inside. Each section of the spine had different colored linoleum so you could identify your location.

On paper, I was adequately trained for my chaplaincy at the county jail, but there was nothing like experience to teach you the ministry. At master control, I had been given a beeper. "Just press the button if you have trouble with an inmate. We'll get help to you immediately. Be prepared to lie on the floor on your stomach so the responding officers can see the word 'Chaplain' on the back of your shirt. They need to be able to separate the sheep from the goats in a hurry." Great, I thought, a Bible comedian in master control.

During my first visit, I was the observer while Vergene taught the lesson. Later, we headed back up the spine toward master control. I was still clumsy with the electronics, and I pushed the panic button inadvertently. As it turned out, the spine was lined with loudspeakers and cameras. "Ms. Smith," a pleasant voice said, "did you activate your security alarm?" Two city blocks away, through the glass doors and windows, I could see the officer who spoke to me. I'd only been in the jail for about an hour, and I nearly had the SWAT team coming to my rescue.

That December morning, we let ourselves into the administrative office and started filling out the paper work. I showed Vergene my song sheets. "They approved my Christmas carols, so we can take them up this morning and sing a few songs."

She nodded, and we filled our bag with New Testaments. Yellow slips of paper and golf pencils were added for the inmates' prayer requests. I located the sheet where we recorded each woman's name and birth date. They received credit at their release hearing if they attended the chaplains' classes. We taught the Bible lessons upstairs in what they called the conference room. Newly arrived inmates started out there, getting their orientation into jail life.

When all the details were taken care of, Vergene and I bowed our heads and thanked the Lord for the open door He had given us in the jail.

The deputy in pod two answered the phone and said that we could come up. We waited as master control opened the transparent doors one at a time. Finally, we were inside, and I could hear the deputy announcing over the loudspeaker, "Bible study in the conference room. Come on down if you want to attend Bible study in the conference room."

The women began to trickle in, one by one. It was an average-sized class that day—about six. For the inmates, it was a choice between a shower and Bible study. I admired them for making a difficult decision. I glanced out at the rest of the general population who weren't attending our class. Some headed for the showers, while others walked in circles in the small exercise area. Several lined up at the two pay telephones on the wall. If friends or family deposited money in their account, they could buy communication with the outside.

A young woman named Julie joined our group and sat down in a chair by the door. I had met her once before, and I knew she was mentally ill. When I approached her to put her name on the list, I could tell why she was seated apart from the others. For her, the decision between showering and attending our class had been easy. It was obvious she hadn't bathed for several days.

When the state closed the mental hospital in our area thirteen years ago, there was no place left for many of society's most vulnerable members. Often, their erratic behavior landed them in jails all over the tri-county area.

Julie's questions erupted like rapid fire. "Does this class go up till lunch? Will we be here until lunch? What time is lunch?"

I gave her a New Testament. "That's okay," she said and handed it back. "I don't need it."

When I described the snow to the group, they all fell silent, and I saw more than a few tears. The hardest part

23

of jail was being separated from their children, and they knew how excited their kids would be about the snow.

"Before we start," I said, "I thought we'd sing a few Christmas carols."

"That's right, we've only got seventeen shopping days until Christmas," Rita called out. We all laughed.

"Can we sing 'O Holy Night'?" Julie asked in a loud voice.

The laughter stopped abruptly, and we all stared at her.

"I want to sing 'O Holy Night.'"

Glancing quickly at Vergene, I nodded and began to sing, but Julie interrupted me. "That's too high. It's got to be lower."

The others snickered. They had been coping with Julie for several days. Mentally ill inmates were usually at the bottom of the quickly established pecking order.

"Okay," I said. "You choose a key."

As she began to sing, not only the women in the class stared in amazement, but I could see most of the others outside in the pod turn to listen. Julie sang out strong in a lovely, low contralto voice, and she knew every word. "Till He appeared and the soul felt its worth . . ."

She gazed out ahead of her, fixing her eyes on something the rest of us couldn't see. "Fall on your knees! O hear the angel voices!"

Julie had a history of hearing inner voices, but that morning in pod two she seemed to be listening to the voice of her Shepherd as she sang about the night He was born. He had obviously shown her the value of her soul.

A holy silence lingered in the conference room as her final notes trailed away. In this cold, steel-barred institution with color-coded linoleum, we had been visited by the powerful story of our Savior. Like the Magi, Julie had offered a gift to the Lord—and delivered it with love.

—*Molly Smith*

Christmas Canceled

The Lord will guide you continually,
giving you water when you are dry
and restoring your strength.
You will be like a well-watered garden,
like an ever-flowing spring.
ISAIAH 58:11

I held back my tears that Christmas morning, determined to listen contentedly as Jesus spoke to me. I was home alone, having been widowed three years earlier. My husband's elderly parents couldn't handle the loss or provide any comfort for me; their lives had been ravaged by Alzheimer's disease.

I had planned to spend Christmas with my son and his wife. They had recently moved to a city three hour's drive from me, but the snow had come in merciless waves, burying our area in several feet of white. The snowplows couldn't keep up. Although I longed to be with family for Christmas, Jesus burdened my heart against traveling. The kids were disappointed. Staring through misty eyes at my Christmas tree, I recalled holidays past, when all of us gathered together. It would never happen again. Life seemed dark and dry.

As I bowed my head to receive the Lord's guidance, I sensed Him prompting me to prepare for the trip. Was

I hearing correctly? Fresh snow had fallen overnight, and the clouds looked threatening. Would traveling be wise? A second prompt convinced me. I jumped to my feet and began packing. As I finished, the sun emerged to show itself for the first time in days, and the snow started melting.

I called my son quickly to say I was on the way. Unrestrained laughter revealed his delight that God had freed me to come. The roads were cleared, and the sun shone majestically for much of the trip. I praised God for His guidance.

When I arrived, my son and his wife couldn't have been happier to see me. They were newlyweds, just transferred to a new city and living in a new home sadly absent of furniture. They had just discovered their first child was on the way. The kids were overwhelmed and frightened.

Jesus gave me the words to comfort them: testimonies of His faithfulness. Peace filled their home, as they drank in refreshing truths. Meanwhile ceaseless snow continued outside.

Three days later, Jesus prompted me to leave. Once again, I traveled in sunshine, this time rejoicing in the refreshment God had brought to both me and my family.

Thank God for His guidance and His refreshment; so abundant, it overflows to others.

—*Laura L. Bradford*

December 4
A Change of Perspective

My stepfather was a good man in spite of the fact that he didn't believe in educating girls. On this subject, he was adamant. "All a girl does with her life is get married and have babies. You don't need an education for that." He added that if I went to high school, I'd have to pay my own way. I looked to my mother for support since her parents had forced her to drop out once she finished eighth grade. However, she was a quiet and submissive woman, and she expressed no opinion. Even without her encouragement, I was determined to continue my education.

I was just fourteen years old in the summer of 1943, when I walked down Capitol Street in Charleston, West

Virginia, looking for work. I saw a sign in the window of The Outlet, a dress shop located across the street from Scott Drug Store: "Wanted, part-time cashier and bookkeeper." I took the sign from the window and walked inside where a short, thickset man met me. Looking over the top of the gold-rimmed glasses that rested on his nose, Mr. Abraham Wolfe asked in a friendly manner if he could be of help.

I handed him the sign. "I'd like to have this job," I said. "I can work after school during the week, all day on Saturdays, and full-time during the summers. And I can start right away."

A dubious expression appeared on his face. Perhaps he saw me a pitiful little waif. With some hesitation, he handed me an application form and said he'd "give it a try." After he looked over the completed form, he asked, "You're only fourteen years old?"

"Yes, Sir," I replied, "but I can get a work permit down the street at the Social Security office if you will sign a paper—I've already checked on it. Besides, I'll be fifteen years old later this month, and in another year, I'll no longer need a work permit."

"Okay," he replied. "It might work. We're open from nine to nine all summer long, and you can start work next Monday. My employees call me 'The Boss.'" He filled out the special form I would need to obtain a work permit, handed it to me, and I ran down Capitol Street to the Social Security office.

"You're the second one in this morning," the clerk greeted me. "More and more young folk under sixteen are seeking jobs—you're fortunate to have found this one." I would discover later how true those heartening words were to me.

On Monday, Mr. Wolfe introduced me to the other six employees—all much older than I—and they welcomed me into "the family" at The Outlet. That summer, I learned how to operate the cash register and balance the books. During the school years that followed, I walked from Woodrow Wilson Junior High, and later from Stonewall Jackson High, to The Outlet each afternoon, where I would close the cash register and balance the books.

I grew to love my newfound family, and they took me under their wing. On my sixteenth birthday in June 1945, when I no longer needed a work permit, they surprised me with a party. I was overcome with emotion because they had thought to make that day so very special to me. I knew I was a very fortunate young girl. I made straight A's in school, I earned sixty cents an hour at The Outlet, and Ted, my steady date, had given me a "pre-engagement" ring.

By June 1945, the war was over, but during the year before, word had begun to leak out from Europe that Hitler had tried to eliminate the Jewish people. "By the end of the War," our local *Charleston Gazette* reported, "there may not be one Jew left in Europe." The Boss had dozens of relatives in Germany, and little information was forthcoming. He feared all of his siblings and cousins had perished. Our usually jolly Boss became withdrawn and sad, so the seven of us set out to see if we could make the December holidays extra special for him.

One of the clerks, Mrs. Cohen, was also Jewish. I was completely naive when it came to knowing how the Jews celebrated Christmas, or if they acknowledged the holiday at all. I asked her about it, and for the first time in my life, I heard the story of Chanukah. I learned that the Jewish people would have been wiped off the face of the earth by the Syrian king, Antiochus, had God not stepped in and saved them. Once King Antiochus was defeated, the Temple, which the wicked man had defiled, needed to be cleansed. The ritual required an eight-day supply of oil for the lamps, but only a one-day supply of oil was available. The Jews needed a miracle if the Temple was to be rededicated.

Mrs. Cohen told me that the Book of Maccabees in the Bible describes how the small amount of oil miraculously lasted for the whole eight days of the cleansing ritual. Chanukah became known as the "Miracle of the Lights."

"Chanukah will begin the last day of November this year, and will last eight days," she said. "Maybe we could have a Chanukah party for The Boss?" All of us agreed enthusiastically, and we planned the party.

31

Mrs. Cohen taught us the loosely translated words to a thirteenth-century Yiddish song, "Maoz Tzur" to sing for The Boss. His wife and Mrs. Cohen fixed special treats for the occasion, and on Friday evening, November twenty-ninth, all of the employees were ready when the store closed. As Mr. Wolfe approached the door of the back room of the store, we began to sing.

Rocky Fortress of my Salvation, It is delightful to praise You.
Restore Thy Holy Temple, and we'll give thanks with an offering
Then we'll complete with a song of hymn, the dedication of the Temple.

Who can retell the things that befell us, who can count them all?
When Maccabeus, our hero and sage, came to our aid. Who can retell the things that befell us, who can count them all?
For in every age a hero or sage has came to our aid.

Chanukah is a great holiday. We'll eat our torte and cakes.
Chanukah is a great holiday. We'll spin the Dreidel with joy.
A big miracle happened there. All the lamps were lit there.

A holiday of happiness, as we celebrate this miracle of lights.

Tears trickled down The Boss' face as he stood speech-less in the doorway, but he made an effort to regain his composure as we sang the chorus again. We laughed and hugged one another before we devoured the latkes, tortes, and matzoh meal apple cake. Nothing in this world was worth more than this moment to me—watching my boss respond to our love and respect for him.

I've had many "unforgettable moments" in my life-time, but this one ranks right up there with the best. From my first day of work in June 1943, until I graduated from Stonewall Jackson High School in May 1947, Mr. and Mrs. Wolfe and all the employees at The Outlet treated me with kindness and respect. It was with great sadness that I moved on after graduation. I accepted a position as lab technician at Commercial Testing and Engineering, a job that The Boss had encouraged me to take. Of course, he wished me well.

It came as no surprise that, as a Christian, my own celebration of Christmas changed after that party in 1945. I realized that without the miracle of Chanukah, there would be no miracle of Christmas. Surely, the "Mir-acle of Lights" from the Chanukah oil, and the miracle of the Light from the Star of Behlehem were from the same source—Jehovah God. For the Jewish people, Chanukah is the celebration of the miracle when the Jews cleansed their Temple. For me, the Star of Bethlehem announced the birth of Jesus Christ, the Lamb of God. Our Savior was born in a stable, but what better place is there for a Lamb to be born?

—*Evelyn Rhodes Smith*

The Annual Christmas Letter

Every time I think of you, I give thanks to my God.
Philippians 1:3

A friend and I compared our Christmas to-do lists over a cup of coffee. "Buy stamps" was at the top of mine, and I asked her if she wanted me to pick up a roll for her too.

"I don't send Christmas cards," she said. "I don't believe in writing a generic letter, and I don't have time to write something special to everyone. Besides, it's expensive."

I was a bit surprised she felt this way, and later that weekend, even more surprised to read that a popular etiquette expert listed "Skip the Christmas cards" in her column of helpful holiday stress-busting tips. She assured readers that this would not be impolite.

Her suggestion may not break any etiquette rules, but we need Christmas cards. More importantly, we need the support and encouragement they bring, the smiles they create, and the memories they refresh.

Consider the letters the Apostle Paul wrote to Christians in Rome, Corinth, Galatia, Ephesus, Philippi, and Thessalonica. He began each letter with a warm welcome that emphasized God's grace and the unmerited blessings given to those who believe in Christ. Then, he gave thanks for the community's faith, their diligence in remaining true to the gospel, and their friendship.

Each of Paul's letters addressed specific issues of conflict or concern occurring within the communities, but when read closely, it's easy to see he wrote them with love and a sincere interest in those who would read and hear them. His words reminded Christians of their relationship with one another and encouraged them to look to each other for strength.

That's what I hope to accomplish with my Christmas letters. I want family and friends to know that I count them among my blessings, that I remember them and the times we spent together, and that I pray for them.

In return, I don't expect expensive, glittery cards with fancy script or a four-page epistle filled with details of the year's activities. Still, I do appreciate the note that says, "Merry Christmas. I'm praying for you, too."

Grace and peace to you from God our Father and the Lord Jesus Christ.

—Karna Converse

December 5
Great Expectations

Every Christmas season, when we decorate our tree, we unwrap each ornament and talk about what makes it special. "I bought this when I was pregnant with you, Ryan," I said to my oldest son as I handed him the "Great Expectations" ornament. It was only fitting that he hung this ornament because I bought it the year my husband and I were anticipating his birth. Like all first-time parents, we were full of hope and anticipation as we awaited the arrival of the person that would change our lives.

On the threshold of bringing a baby into the world, my husband and I viewed life through the lens of optimism. What would our child be like? What great things would he accomplish? How would our family be enriched and blessed by his presence? We could hardly wait to find out. I could only imagine how Mary and Joseph must have felt as they anticipated the birth of Jesus Christ—the one who would truly change the world for all mankind.

I purchased a hand-crafted ornament featuring a loving couple holding hands as they smiled down at her obvious pregnancy. The expressions on their faces echoed the banner above over them which read, "Great Expectations." That Christmas, I placed this ornament in the center of our tiny tree.

Our son was born shortly after the Christmas decorations were tucked away in the attic, and we quickly forgot about our great expectations as we fought to keep him alive. He suffered from an incurable liver disease, combined with severe food allergies and asthma. We faced one battle after another, month after month, year after year. We spent one Christmas in the hospital as Ryan struggled to break through a bout with asthma. Each breath was a struggle as his little lungs fought for air. His heart rate raced out of control from the medicine used to clear his lungs.

"Isn't his heart rate too high?" I asked the nurse.

She hesitated before answering. "Yes, but if he can't breathe, it won't beat at all."

At home, we decorated the tree, and the "Great Expectations" ornament still took center stage. I prayed for God's hand to touch Ryan's lungs, and I clung to the promises in

His Word. God's faithfulness sustained us, and He demonstrated His power in true miracles and healings. However, those years were hard on us in many ways. We struggled financially, but God always made sure our needs were met. Our health weakened from the stress, and our marriage suffered, too. We were strained and exhausted with little time for each other, but we persevered. We were determined to cling to our hopes and dreams for our family.

The trials did not end once our son was healthy. After a period of rest and peace, we found ourselves in another battle. A bizarre accident involving a lightning strike and electrocution set off a series of health problems that plagued my husband for years. He suffered from depression and chronic pain, but doctors, specialists, and medical tests failed to provide an accurate diagnosis or treatment. The domino effect was felt by everyone in the family. There were times when I wondered how we would keep our family together. Once again, the great expectations I had treasured seemed to be hidden along with the Christmas decorations.

Each year, when I unwrapped the ornament of the smiling husband and pregnant wife, I would think back to the time when everything seemed bright and nothing felt impossible for us. The message of great expectations continued to remind me that God's mercies were new each day. Over time, that ornament became more than a memento of the year we waited for our first child. It evolved into a memorial of everything God had done for us. It became a symbol of hope—hope for the future and a lasting reminder that God makes all things possible.

Our family expanded with another son, and we continued to add to our collection until the "Great Expectations" ornament was just one of many. Last Christmas, as I hung it on the tree, I noticed it looked more worn than I had seen it in the past. The young bride's hair was a bit disheveled, and the groom was bald. She was missing a hand, and her husband's face was scraped and chewed from one of our dogs. Even the banner declaring their motto for their life was broken, but I could still read the words, "Great Expectations."

Time had taken its toll on the ornament, just as it had on our lives. I pondered this for a few minutes and wondered if I should laugh or cry. I chose to laugh because the ornament was still a symbol of our lives. We may have been a bit weathered from our tests and trials, but we were still holding each other. Maybe we had learned to adjust our expectations, but we still had hope and anticipation of good things for our life together. We had discovered that life can be hard, but God is forever faithful. We were still together, and we were still building our family and creating wonderful memories.

The baby born at the first Christmas is the reason we can hang on when life gets tough and threatens to destroy us. For thousands of years, the world had eagerly awaited

God's promise of redemption and new life. His people knew about great expectations, for they had listened to the prophecies of Christ's birth for generations.

This Christmas, our family has one more reason to celebrate because we received, yet again, another miracle. After more than ten years of suffering and misdiagnosis, the source of my husband's pain was discovered. The problem was corrected, and he is on his way to regaining his zest for life. This year, as we placed the ornaments on the tree, he announced that he "had a bounce in his step" for the first time in many years.

We know that one day all pain, all fear, and all tears will be wiped away when we enter our eternal home, but for now, we hold on to the hope that does not disappoint. We have learned that great expectations are not fulfilled by our own power and strength, but through the one who is the author of all hope and expectation—our Savior Jesus Christ.

—*Mary Gallagher*

God Left His Mark

I look up to the mountains—does my help come from there?
My help comes from the Lord who made heaven and earth!
PSALM 121:1–2

It was the day after Christmas. No sooner had my husband, Bill, and I opened our gifts than we were wrapping them up again for the long trip to our new home 500 miles away. Our new apartment was in a valley surrounded by mountains, a stark contrast to the beach community that we once called home. I felt uncertain about the many differences in our new setting, and I worried I would be unable to adjust to so much change.

Distracted by the duties of setting up house and the remnants of the holiday season, my concerns were temporarily forgotten. Yet, when the last of the Christmas decorations were packed away, I found myself in the midst of post-holiday blues. As I looked out at the icy, white sky that settled over the valley every morning, I felt homesick and alone.

"Take a ride around town," Bill suggested. "You'll feel better."

It was going to take a lot more than a joy ride to help me out of my funk, I thought. Yet, I set out to explore the neighborhood, and under a steady drizzle, I drove to the downtown area. By the time I reached the local supermarket, the heavens opened and released a torrential rain. I parked my car and ran inside for a few items, although navigating the unfamiliar aisles quickly became an exercise in frustration. "I'll never get used to this town," I muttered as I exited with my purchases.

I put down my head against the chill evening wind. At least it had stopped raining. "Just take a look at that beautiful sky," a friendly older gentleman said as he placed the last of his groceries in his trunk and closed the hatch. "God certainly left His mark there."

I looked up. Just beyond the tips of the mountains, the charcoal clouds parted, and the sun was setting amid bright gold, orange, and purple streaks. It was a sight more magnificent than any holiday lights, and it served as a reminder that the Lord was with me always. With His help, I would soon adjust to my new surroundings.

We are surrounded by the miraculous evidence of God's creation.

—Monica A. Andermann

December 6
The Faith of a Child

$\mathcal{T}$he Christmas lights of Salt Lake City sparkled that night, and the town looked as if it had been touched by angels. However, by morning the weatherman's report for north-central Utah sounded far from heavenly. "Winter storm watch in effect," he repeated throughout the day.

It was early December, 1985. We had enjoyed a weekend of touring the city's holiday displays with our nine-year-old-son, Davey, but the thought of being caught in a blizzard troubled me. "Do you think we should head home right away to avoid the storm?" I asked my husband, Russ.

He cocked his balding head and glanced at the gunmetal gray clouds above. "The weatherman has a fifty-fifty chance of being correct, so I vote for eating at Ho Ho's Chinese and then leaving. The snow probably won't start until later."

Tiny warning bells rang in my head. "It's a two-hour drive; go *now*."

A cold wind plucked at our clothing. I pulled Davey's jacket tighter around him and smoothed his blond cowlick with my fingertips. "We could grab a burger at a drive-through and leave now, so we'd be closer to home when bad weather hits."

Davey's blue eyes pleaded with me. "Can't we at least stay long enough to eat Chinese food?"

Russ chimed in. "You know you're dying to eat Moo Goo Gai Pan. It won't take very long at the restaurant."

The warning bells continued to peal, repeating the same admonition. I gazed at the sky. Was that a tiny snowflake I felt? I wiped my cheek—it seemed dry. I must have imagined it. Looking at my family's happy faces, I didn't have the heart to insist on leaving. Instead, I mentally reached over and with a click, turned off the warning bells.

At Ho Ho's, the pungent smell of sweet and sour enticed us to stay. The restaurant was crowded, and we waited and waited for a table. When the food came, it was delicious, but it would have tasted even better if I hadn't felt so uneasy. "Can you eat a little faster?" I asked Davey, as he played with the rice on his plate. I fidgeted in my seat. "Russ, we really should leave. Let's ask for a doggy bag and take the rest of the food home."

With the remainder of our meal in cardboard boxes, we walked out of the restaurant and came to an abrupt stop, stunned by the scene in front of us. Huge snowflakes whipped about as the wind blew them into drifts, while the tire tracks from cars looked like indecipherable scrawls imprinted on the snow-covered avenues. My mind filled with dread at the sight. Despite the fact that I had tried to turn the bells off earlier, they now clanged, "You should've listened."

We climbed into the car, and Russ turned on the radio as we drove to the Interstate. In between songs, the announcer continually warned people to stay home, or to carry emergency equipment in their cars if they needed to travel.

Once on the highway, my heart clenched as the air around us became a blanket of white, and visibility dropped to one-hundred feet. Despite the hazardous conditions, cars passed us, throwing slush all over the windshield of our little Chevy Chevette.

Russ leaned forward, peering intently and trying to see through the ice that formed under the wipers. I leaned with him, hoping to help. In the back seat, Davey sang and talked, oblivious to the danger.

The snow fell harder. Visibility decreased, and although we were on a major freeway, traffic slowed to thirty miles an hour. Then, the car in front of us slid, and Russ hit the brakes.

Wham! Our seatbelts caught with a jerk as a vehicle behind slammed into the Chevette. Russ looked at Davey and me, his green eyes filled with worry. "Is everyone all right?" When we nodded, he gave a relieved sigh and put his hand on the door handle. "I'd better survey the damage and get insurance information."

Suddenly, I had a vision of Russ stepping out to check over the Chevette, and being hit by sliding vehicles that bounced off each other like billiard balls. This time, I didn't ignore the warning. "Don't, Russ. There could be a forty-car pileup at any minute, and you'd be killed. It doesn't matter if the car is dented. As long as it's drivable, let's keep going."

Russ stepped on the gas and we crept forward along the snow-encrusted road. I hoped no one else would run into us—especially an eighteen-wheeler. I had always wondered how someone could shake with fear, and for the first time in my life, I found out. I couldn't stop the small tremors of anxiety that vibrated me from head to foot as I focused on the highway.

"Mom," Davey said, breaking my concentration.

"Not now, Sweetie. I have to help Dad watch the road so we don't wreck." Silence reigned, and I turned my attention back to the car ahead. Abruptly, it fishtailed, spun in circles, and slid into the median. The driver appeared unhurt, but we didn't dare stop for fear of being rear-ended again—or worse, smashed flat by a truck. However, with no taillights visible in front of us, it was impossible to tell if we were driving down the middle of the highway or about to fall off the edge of an exit ramp.

Davey tapped the back of my seat. "Mom, I need to tell you something."

"Not *now!*" I said, through teeth chattering with fear. "Davey, I told you Dad and I can't talk right now."

For a split second, Davey said nothing. Then his young voice softly floated from the back. "But Mom, we need to say a prayer and ask Jesus to get us home safe."

Russ nodded in agreement, yet kept his attention on the road. "That's a great idea. Mom and I can't close our eyes, so you go ahead and say one out loud for us."

At that moment, I couldn't help but think of Matthew 21:15: "The leading priests and the teachers of religious law ... heard even the children in the Temple shouting, 'Praise God for the Son of David.'" It had taken the child among us to acknowledge Jesus Christ's divine power, and to suggest praying for the protection we desperately needed.

Davey recited a sweet, simple prayer that came from the heart, and I relished its calming effect immediately. Although still apprehensive, I felt better than before and offered up a silent prayer of my own.

Ice and snow continued to accumulate on the edges of the windshield, making the Chevette feel like a coffin. We looked for an exit, hoping to stop and clear off the car, but falling snow obliterated road signs. Finally, in an attempt to improve visibility, Russ and I opened our windows, unbuckled our seat belts, and with Russ still driving, leaned out as far as we could reach and brushed the snow off the edges of the front window. No doubt, Davey's prayer kept us from wrecking the car in the process.

As we approached Point of the Mountain, near Draper, the visibility decreased again. Snow blew in a swirling ground blizzard, and then suddenly, a shape loomed in the road. "Watch out," I cried. "There's something ahead."

Russ hit the brakes. He struggled to control the skidding, and we finally slowed to a stop. A man stood in the middle of the highway, waving his arms. He ran to the driver's side, and Russ rolled down his window. I glanced out the back with dread. What if another vehicle didn't see us in time and plowed into the Chevette?

Snow blew in as the man said, "My car is stuck in the left lane. I can't get it started again. My wife and baby are inside. Can you give us a ride to Provo?"

Russ nodded. "Hurry and get in, before we get hit."

Davey scooted over while the family climbed in beside him. Our little compact car now held six people. After chatting for a few minutes, the guy said, "This is one of the worst storms I've ever seen."

"Yes," Davey replied, "but I said a prayer so we all will get home okay." Everyone smiled, but I could almost hear sighs of relief, too.

When I look back on our terrifying winter adventure, I know that Davey's prayers and faith protected not only his own family, but the family that rode with us also found themselves enfolded in the arms of our Savior. Praise belongs to the Lord, from whom all blessings flow—the One whose birth it was then, and forever will be, a privilege to celebrate.

—*Cindy Beck*

What's It All About?

Why am I discouraged?
Why is my heart so sad?
I will put my hope in God!
I will praise him again—
my Savior and my God!
PSALM 42:11

Bells were ringing, lights were twinkling, and parties were in full swing. It seemed everyone was happy—everyone except me. The truth was I wished the holiday season had been over. I still had shopping to do and errands to run, my energy was depleted, and my bank balance was dwindling. I was wondering, what was this all about anyway?

In the midst of a stressful season, the holiday blues had crept in. After reading articles and searching the Internet, I've learned that it was common for seniors to experience depression during the holiday season. I could blame it on aching joints and other health problems, lack of money, or family troubles. However, I decided that the real culprits were the thoughts I allowed to dominate my thinking.

My sadness and discontent began with a single negative thought that invariably led to more. My health was failing. I was becoming more dependent on others. Everybody else was busy. No one cared about me.

Maybe I succumbed to the Santa Claus mentality and subscribed to the myth that Santa visited everyone but me. Sometimes I thought the whole world was having a party, and I had been left without an invitation. When this happened, I knew I allowed myself and my feelings to become the center of my attention. I had forgotten the one whose birthday was the origin of this grand celebration.

Many of God's great servants had bouts of depression and overcame their despair with the help of the Lord. Jeremiah, Elijah, and David all experienced "the dark night of the soul." In 1 Samuel 30:6, I discovered David's answer to discouragement: "David was now in serious trouble because his men were very bitter, and they began to talk of stoning him. But David found strength in the Lord his God."

Just as David did, I have found power and positive thinking in the Lord. Christmas is now a time to shift my focus from my circumstances to the miraculous gift that God placed in a manger on that first Christmas.

I will pull away from the noise and clamor to center my thoughts on Jesus the Savior.

—*Virginia Dawkins*

December 7
Something Unexpected from Santa

We were much too big to sit on Santa's lap, and we knew the guy in the red suit wasn't visiting from the North Pole. He was just an older, white-haired gentleman from the neighborhood, paid to entertain kids. We were just two giggly, twelve-year-old girls anticipating the gift that Santa's little helper would give us for a quick visit with the old man.

Crystal and I were still closet Barbie doll players, something we pinky-swore we wouldn't tell anyone else in our class. Playing dolls was considered pretty passé by then. We concluded the other girls were much too busy acting hard-to-get with the boys or playing organized sports on the weekends to still play with dolls.

In an attempt to rationalize our trip to Santa, we decided if we got a free doll, the standard little girl gift, we'd have something to do for the weekend. We also wanted to relive a bit of the magic that believing in Santa and standing in line to see him used to make us feel. All I knew was that I wasn't quite ready to be completely grown up.

As we towered over the toddler in front of us, we laughed at our goofy endeavor. My mother had finally relented, rolled her eyes, and left her little comedians to do a little shopping while we waited in line. When it was our turn, we grinned at the guy who was about to get a little heavier load on his lap than usual.

"Well, come on up," Santa said. So, Crystal and I made our way to the brightly decorated throne to acknowledge a man in whom we had long ago stopped believing.

"Hello girls," he said in a booming voice. Then, he began to whisper so the other kids wouldn't hear. "I figure you're too old to believe in Santa anymore, but why don't you tell me what you're wishing for this Christmas?"

Crystal and I glanced at each other and thought about our answers. We knew this guy wouldn't bring us the hair styler that instantly twisted your hair and adorned it with beads, or the cool, florescent-striped bike shorts all the girls were wearing in gym class. We knew we had to ask our parents if we wanted to see any of these things under the tree.

"Well, why don't you ask for our troops to stay safe for the holidays," Santa said.

"Yeah, that's a good one," Crystal replied.

He smiled. "How about world peace?"

"Definitely!" we replied.

"Well, you know what?" he said, "World peace starts with you."

I began to sober up a bit from the giddiness of our little exploit, and judging from the expression on Crystal's face, she did too.

As we looked dumbfounded at one another, Santa said, "It does begin with you. It's those little acts you do every day that promote peace."

At that point, Crystal and I couldn't think of anything worthwhile to say, so we just listened as the old man continued, "It might be as simple as helping someone who dropped something, or you could donate time tutoring another student. All these things make the world a better place. There's no simple solution to achieving world peace, and there's no single person who can make it happen alone. Keeping our troops safe starts with you too, you know. All you have to do is say a little prayer for them."

I began to seriously mull over what he was saying. I couldn't believe how this mall Santa, a regular local guy, going along with our stunt, had turned into some kind of philosopher. Shrouded by all the insecurities and self-obsession of adolescence, we hadn't even considered how our little acts could make a difference for the world as a whole. What could be more important to ask for at Christmas? For a moment, those portable CD players and computer games appeared petty and superfluous in the larger scope.

"I hadn't even thought about it like that," Crystal said.

"It's true," Santa replied. "Peace can't start without you, and prayers can't be heard until they're actually prayed. People might even see what you're doing, and it will brighten their day. The people you help will certainly be grateful. They may even be inspired to do their own kind acts. And little by little, fighting and violence will have no place in this world."

He paused to look us both in the eyes. Behind his tacked-on mask and plastic eyeglasses, we saw genuine sincerity. "I hope you girls do think about it when you go home today. Say a little prayer and do a few nice things today— and every day." We nodded our assent, and I silently vowed to be a little nicer.

As our minds stirred with the significance of what he had said, we thanked Santa, and an assistant handed us our wrapped gifts. We had nearly forgotten about them. Feeling a bit guilty, I saw our scheme to score free gifts as rather pointless. Now, the wrapping paper and blister packs seemed cheapened by our childish self-interest, their value trivialized by what we had just heard.

Not long ago, around Christmastime, I received a phone call from a woman who was looking for someone whose name I didn't recognize. Through the congestion of a cold, I promptly told her she had the wrong number. As my finger went to cancel the call, she asked if I was feeling all right. We enjoyed a short, friendly chat, and when it was over, she wished me a Merry Christmas and offered to say a prayer for my cold.

That brief incident reminded me once more of the Santa I had met so many years ago. I thought of how complete strangers could have a significant impact on your life by simply offering advice or a small prayer. Both Santa and the woman on the phone gave up a few moments of their time to try and make the world a better place. I couldn't help but wonder about my potential impact on someone's life, perhaps by saying a little prayer, sharing a smile, or helping to build a house for their family.

I can't remember what was in those packages Crystal and I received from Santa's helper so long ago, but it doesn't matter. In a forty-hour week filled with screaming children, flailing diaper bags, and temper tantrums, a patient stranger was good-humored enough to indulge our frivolous act and thoughtful enough to send us away with a special gift. He gave us something we never even thought to ask for, but it was something that brought back the spirit and magic of Christmas.

—*Jessica Collins*

A Son Is Given

For God loved the world so much that he gave his one and only Son, so that everyone who believes in him will not perish but have eternal life.

JOHN 3:16

How would you react if someone gave you their son? What would you do if they gave you their beloved child? One chilly winter morning, my husband and I sat across a table in a public library from a young woman who was giving us her newborn son through adoption. She was about to entrust him to our care for the rest of his life.

I thought I would cry; instead, I was stunned by the magnitude of the woman's selfless act. What does one say to someone who has given a gift of such immense magnitude? How can one truly fathom the depth of that sacrifice, or comprehend the full power of such a love?

I sat in silence and listened as she described the pain that led to this difficult choice. I watched as she held back tears and recalled the last time she had held her child. I saw her struggle to capture the depth of her love for her little boy with mere words. "Time to go," announced the social worker. Already? Now? Just like that?

In less than an hour, an amazing transaction had taken place. Two moms parted with one last embrace, and a transfer of love occurred. I fumbled for something brilliant to say, but no Hallmark moment came to mind.

"Thank you," I breathed at last. The phrase sounded awkward and pathetic. I had just been given a human life. I felt so unworthy.

Our joy came at a terrible price. No money could repay our debt; no words could heal her loss. Yet, every day, we could choose to love her son with all our hearts, souls, minds, and strength. In doing so, we would honor the giver of this most precious gift. So, we made a promise, sealed our commitment with signatures on a dotted line, and welcomed our son into our hearts for eternity.

Never forget that our joy this Christmas comes from the greatest, most powerful gift of all—the gift of a Son.

—*Katherine Ryan Craddock*

December 8
The Christmas
I Almost Missed

My daughter watched me hurriedly clean the silver after I put another batch of cookies into the oven. "Mom, I'm worried about you," she said. "You seem so stressed lately."

I sighed. "I'll be fine. I just want this Christmas to be special."

"Well, I can at least help you with the cleaning this afternoon."

I was determined to make Christmas 1972 our biggest and best Christmas ever. My daughter Mary Beth was getting married the following February, and this would be her last Christmas at home. She was the last of my three children to leave the nest. I would be alone after that, for the first time in my life.

Through the years, Mary Beth had been my friend, as well as my daughter. Sometimes, single moms grow closer to their children as they face the world together without a husband and father in the household. So, when she and her fiancé, Don, announced their engagement that fall, it was a bittersweet moment. I was happy for them, but I felt sad for myself.

I wasn't ready to let my daughter go or to live alone, so I coped by focusing all my attention and energies on "The Gala Production"—the last Christmas with our small family still intact. It would be even more special that year because my parents had recently moved from Chicago to California to be near us. My two sons were also joining us for the holiday, making the family circle complete.

I started planning our Christmas celebration in November, and by early December I had worked myself into a frenzy. By mid-December, I was a basket case. There were all those perfect presents to shop for, and the apartment would have to be spotless, as well as exquisitely decorated. I was also busy writing notes on Christmas cards, baking cookies, and planning the Christmas menu, all while holding down a full-time job.

Because of my impossible, self-imposed schedule, I grew more tired with each passing day. I was stressed to the limits of my endurance, and I didn't have time for anything except going to work and getting ready for Christmas. A regular churchgoer, I couldn't even find time to go to church during the month of December.

On the last Sunday before Christmas, I woke up exhausted. I started to roll over and go back to sleep, but something in my spirit urged me to get up and go to church that morning. I realized I had missed hearing all the old, beloved Christmas carols, so I dragged my weary body out of bed and hurried off to church, arriving slightly late. I could hear the congregation singing as I slipped inside and found a seat near the back.

I sat there for a moment while I focused on the lyrics in the song. "Oh come, all ye faithful, joyful and triumphant." I slumped in my seat. I wasn't feeling any joy or triumph, and I knew I hadn't even been very faithful lately. I watched while other latecomers marched down the aisles toward some empty places near the front. They all appeared joyful and triumphant, as they assembled to celebrate the birth of our Lord Jesus.

Why didn't I feel that way too? In my efforts to create the perfect Christmas, had I almost forgotten the true meaning of the season? My weary body sagged, along with my spirit, and I began to cry softly. All of my tension and tiredness rose to the surface, and I started to sob uncontrollably. I'm falling apart at the seams, I thought. Still, I couldn't stop crying.

I hadn't even noticed a man sitting next to me, but I was suddenly aware of an arm around my shoulders. I began to cry even harder, but he didn't ask me what was wrong. He seemed to know. Finally, when my sobbing subsided, I blurted out my story. I explained how I had worked so hard to make a memorable holiday for my daughter's last year at home, and how I had almost forgotten what Christmas was all about. Then, I confessed that I had almost missed Christmas. "Please forgive me for making a scene and disturbing you," I said.

"Don't worry about it. You're not disturbing me at all, and you're here now, so you didn't completely forget about worshipping the Lord. If you just keep your eyes on Jesus, everything will be okay. I'm sure you and your family will have a wonderful Christmas."

It was then I noticed his long hair, tie-dyed T-shirt, and rumpled bell bottom jeans. It seemed so incongruous; a conservatively dressed, middle-aged matron being comforted by a hippie about the same age as my sons. Yet, to me, he was a ministering angel.

Suddenly, a feeling of peace settled over me. I dried my eyes, leaned back in my seat, and started to sing along with the congregation. "Joy to the world, the Lord has come, let earth receive her King." I felt the joy, and I whispered a short prayer. "Happy Birthday, Jesus. I'm sorry I almost missed your celebration, but I'm so glad to be here with you now."

At that moment, I realized I would always have a caring, loving family in the church—the body of Christ. I wouldn't be alone when my daughter got married, after all.

Christmas arrived a few days later. It must have been as wonderful as I hoped it would be. I had worked so hard on it. Yet, so many years later, I don't remember much about it. I don't recall how clean my apartment looked, how scrumptious the meal was, or how perfect the gifts were. However, I will never forget that Sunday morning long ago when I rediscovered the true meaning of Christmas.

—*Gay Sorensen*

A Haven of Blessings

God saved you by his grace when you believed. And you can't take credit for this; it is a gift from God.
EPHESIANS 2:8

It's the safe haven of holiday-stressed mothers everywhere. In what other room can the echo of a tiled floor and glow of incandescent bulbs bring so much thoughtfulness and peace?

Not very long ago, the rapidly approaching Christmas letter deadline, piles of unwrapped Christmas presents, and our impending Christmas open house drove me to the recesses of our upstairs bathroom.

Perched atop the lid of my porcelain roost I sat, head in hands, and pondered absolutely nothing. I heard nothing but the faint murmur of Lilly's game of make-believe and the dull din of the college football game my husband was watching. I was free to clear my mind.

It wasn't long before I heard a rustle outside the door. I pulled my face from my hands and turned my head toward the sound. Creeping under the door were four adorable little fingers and a thumb. I smiled and reached down to put my hand on top of his. My one-year-old son giggled.

"Whose hand is this?" I exclaimed in mock outrage. I heard him laugh again. He stuck his hand in further.

Before I knew it, I was cheek to cold floor, gazing under the door into the bright blue eyes of my son. We were both laughing so hard we couldn't stop. We were soon joined by my daughter, and even my husband hit the floor to join in the fun.

It was a powerful moment when my son's attempt to reach me directed me to what was really important. His tiny hand wanted to touch me, while the hand of another child, so many years ago, has touched me in a much more profound way. The hands of Jesus suffered on the cross for you and me, and they still reach out to us today. We get to hold them for an eternity.

My time in the bathroom reminded me that, just as Christ answered Thomas's doubt with an invitation to touch His hands and side, He answers our worry and doubt with an invitation to hold His hand in trust and love.

Be touched by Jesus and feel the peace only He offers.

—*Lauren Jensen*

December 9
Seven Camels and a Wobbly Manger

Every Christmas, my crèche sits on top of Jesse's desk.

Jesse, my mentally handicapped uncle, lived with my husband Tom's family, and his desk, passed on to us at his death, came to Colorado in a covered wagon with their ancestors. It is scarred on top where a bookshelf was attached at one time, but we love its handmade, dovetailed joints and brass drawer handles, carefully crafted by my great-grandfather John Dunsha Steele.

Jesse loved that desk and kept his treasures in it: marbles, old fishing lures he found down at the lake, pieces of driftwood, and pretty rocks. It seemed like the perfect setting for a crèche.

My family came to the St. Vrain Valley of Colorado in a covered wagon, too. When I married Tom, we united two of the oldest families in the valley: the Steeles and the Kiteleys. In the process, we had to figure out how to combine years of separate traditions in our new family. One of the first problems was what to put on top of the tree. My family always used a star, while his preferred an angel. Since we couldn't afford new decorations, I won by default. I had an old star my parents no longer used. When it finally wore out and fell apart, we replaced it with an angel. By then, I'd learned to compromise.

I also brought an old manger scene to the marriage that my artistic mother had passed on to me. She received the figures from her mother, and she used papier-mâché and paint to make a cave-like structure out of an old box to hold the figures. The original set consisted of ceramic figures: Mary, Joseph, Baby Jesus, the three Wise Men, three camels, a shepherd, a donkey, and a wooden manger filled with real hay. I was allowed to play with the pieces as a child. Our old house had hardwood floors, and the donkey, shepherd, sheep, one camel, and Joseph didn't survive my clumsy fingers.

Even Baby Jesus suffered a broken arm, and one leg of the manger ended up shorter than the other three. I loved the set, but as a child, I didn't appreciate its value or significance. I did learn the Christmas story, though, by playing with the pieces and acting out what I'd learned in Sunday school about each figure.

When I inherited the crèche as an adult and wanted to use it for my own family, I tried to find replacements for the broken items when I could afford them. We used to be able to purchase individual figures in "Woolworth's Five and Dime Store," and I found a new Joseph and three sheep that way. A few years later, when I tried again, the only thing available in the right size was made of plastic, so I have a plastic shepherd, donkey, and two camels.

Three wooden camels were added to the collection from a thrift store, and a set of three ceramic pigs arrived when my children were small and insisted that pigs should be in a stable also. "There are pigs on Grandma's farm," they said, "so pigs have to be there to welcome Baby Jesus, too."

My mother's ceramic angel stood on top of the old crèche to watch over the whole scene. She got it in her Christmas stocking when she was a child, and it, too, has been broken and glued back together. It's much too large to go with the other figures, but that's okay. After all, it is an angel.

The old cardboard cave finally disintegrated with age. I didn't have my mother's creative ability to make another one, so I looked for a replacement and found an unpainted wooden crèche stable at a thrift shop. My daughter, who inherited her grandmother's artistic ability, is going to paint it for me someday, but for now, it looks appropriately rustic.

Its roof reminds me of the homes in Germany where we lived for two years. I know it's not historically accurate, but they love Jesus in Germany, too. The big angel has to stand to the side of the scene, since trying to balance her on the roof would probably result in more injuries.

My own children have been more careful with the pieces, and our floor was carpeted when they were growing up, so the figures have not suffered any more indignities since my childhood. They're grown now, but I still put out the crèche each year with all its imperfections and inconsistencies. I'm sure if it didn't appear, I'd hear about it when everyone came for the holidays. There's a new little one in the family now, the start of the next generation, ready to take his turn at loving and, I hope, preserving the crèche.

I like to think we all value the crèche because of the history behind each piece. We don't care if there are seven camels now. Maybe the Wise Men had a whole train of camels to carry their belongings. The pigs still snuggle contentedly in their corner of the stable, and Mary still looks down lovingly at Jesus with his broken arm, teetering in his wobbly manger. We know that much worse would happen to him before his purpose on Earth was fulfilled.

The variety of material reminds me that Jesus loves us all no matter what color we are or what we're made of. Having the crèche from my childhood on top of the old desk from my husband's past reminds me of the marriage vow we took over forty years ago. In one Christmas decoration, I can see back in time to the wagon trains that brought our two separate families to the Saint Vrain Valley to be united in our family. Our story symbolizes the melting pot of America—families leaving their loved ones to start a life with new loved ones.

Once in a while, I think about replacing my crèche. I look at new ones in the stores—all the pieces sparkling clean, intact, and made of the same material. They're beautiful, but I haven't found one that I could imagine replacing mine. Somehow, I don't think I ever will. Like Jesse's desk, it has too much family history, and like the members of my family, I've learned to live with, and even appreciate, all their imperfections. I'm sorry I broke Baby Jesus' arm, but I know he forgives me. After all, that is the real story behind the crèche.

—Jean Campion

A Miracle for Mr. Turner

*The shepherds went back to their flocks, glorifying and
praising God for all they had heard and seen. It was just as
the angel had told them.*
LUKE 2:20

Our church choir was small, and the voices weren't particularly well trained. Despite these limitations, I began
directing a group of would-be musicians in October, as
we practiced music to present to our congregation the
Sunday before Christmas.

The morning of the performance, our phone rang.
"Sorry, we can't make it this morning. It snowed last night
and the pass is blocked." That eliminated two of the best
voices. The phone rang again, and I couldn't recognize the
raspy voice. "There's no way I can sing today. I can hardly
talk." That voice belonged to our soloist.

Even with our choir reduced in number, we went ahead
with the program, but it was not a good performance. I
consoled myself with the thought that, for three months,
we had prayed that the program would be a blessing to our
small congregation.

As I greeted people after the program, Mr. Turner, a
member of the church came to me. "Mrs. Johnson, never

have I heard anything like it. That was the greatest Christmas music I have ever heard."

I stared at him. Had he heard right? Or had something happened between the time the notes left our lips and entered Mr. Turner's ears? A miracle perhaps?

Why not? Isn't that what Christmas is all about: a miracle birth, a miracle star, and miracle music sung to shepherds in the fields? Why not a miracle blessing for Mr. Turner through our less-than-perfect music?

Perhaps you need a miracle this year. Maybe not a musical miracle, but a rocky marriage needs fixing, or you long to be reconciled to a relative who has refused to speak to you all year. Surrounded by mysterious happenings and inexplicable situations, Christmas is a perfect time to believe. So, this December turn your faith loose, hear angels sing, and view a new star in your sky. Like Mary, Joseph, the shepherds, and Mr. Turner, you may very well receive your own Christmas miracle.

Miracles happen every day.

—*Jewell Johnson*

December 10
This Little Light of Mine

The Christmas season was in full swing and we were visiting a local church for their morning worship service. As I belted out the words to the song, "Joy to the World," I couldn't help but smile. How I loved the traditional Christmas carols; the hope and promise their message brings has always rejuvenated my spirit and filled me with peace. What a motivating reminder that our hearts should prepare room for Him—especially during the hectic modern Christmas season in which we live.

The days leading up to the birth of Jesus can almost be an endurance test. One commercial after another tells us the season is all about stuff and money, when in reality the season should be about our focus on God's message of eternal salvation and sharing that message with others.

As we began to sing the second stanza, I glanced at the faces around me, assuming many of them would be full of joy, too. After all, we're Christians; the wonder of the season alone should fill us with such happiness that it couldn't help but spill over onto our faces. Instead, the more I looked, the more disappointed I became. Most of the congregation seemed to be just mouthing the words; you couldn't see "joy" if you stared cross-eyed at them for an hour.

Am I the only one smiling? Am I the only one who feels euphoria that the Lord has come and saved a wretch like me? A few years ago, I heard a cute little saying: If you love the Lord, notify your face. At that moment, looking at the dour faces of this old country congregation, I wanted to shout that little ditty at the top of my lungs. But I never got the chance.

The Lord abruptly reminded me of a time in my own past (He's good at doing that, to make a point), when my sister Sue and I were teenagers. Our mother worked in a department store in the women's sportswear section, and she got great deals on the latest styles for us by using her employee discount on top of sales prices.

Sue's face would light up when she received her new clothes, followed by a squeal of delight over having the latest in fashion. She dashed off to her room to try on her apparel and to see if her new treasures matched other items in her wardrobe. Many times my mother joined her in her room and they'd both get excited over their new discoveries.

While my sister and I are alike in many ways, we do have our differences. Sue has always been slim, and I have almost always been pudgy. Like our mother, she loves to shop for clothes, and they both keep up with the latest fashion. On the other hand, I look at shopping more as a chore, not a joy. The way I see it, clothes are a necessary evil.

As I reflected on this period from my past, I continued glancing at the congregation and their blank faces. My own face was hurting from smiling and singing at the same time; I could have done back flips from the elation erupting inside me. The constant seasonal reminder that I was one of God's kids and would be spending eternity with Him filled my heart with overflowing happiness. Yet, so many others standing with me looked bored. Was worship a "chore" to some people? Were they spiritually pudgy with no interest in decking the halls with smiles of joy?

The irony of the word "appearances" hit home. When I was young, it looked like I wasn't thrilled with my new clothes, even though most of the time I was; mainly because I didn't have to do the shopping. In hindsight, I'm sure my mother was hurt. After all, she had spent her time and money on me, when she didn't have to.

Even as a teenager I could sense her disappointment. I mean, there was my sister, practically doing somersaults, and all Mom got out of me was a low mumble of gratitude. "Are you sure you like them?" she would usually ask, most likely wondering if she had offended me.

"Yeah, they're great. Thanks."

Funny, I almost always liked the selections she made, but even as the words came out of my mouth, I knew they didn't sound very sincere. Instead of dashing to my room to try on the clothes, I would promptly resume whatever it was I had been doing—usually something having to do with books or batter.

Then, something important happened. I recalled how good it made me feel to know my mother was thinking about me and that she spent her time and money to shop for me. Why did she keep doing it? She did it because she loved me and because she knew my personality.

It's the same way with God. He knows us. He knows our joys, and he knows our sorrows. He knows our accomplishments and He knows our failures. He loves us, whether we show our joy or not, and even when we disappoint Him. We are not a surprise to God.

Unexpectedly, I felt convicted of passing judgment on the congregation. Many of them might be elated over the season, but they weren't showing it. For all I knew, there were people in the church, at that very moment, praising God in a humble, quiet way. How could I possibly know what was in their hearts?

For the benefit of those who don't know Jesus on a personal level, we need to let our joy in the Lord show. Our cup should be running over, especially during Christmas, as we allow the significance of the season to fill us with gladness.

The holidays can be exhausting, especially for women who have so much on their plate to balance. While it can be a struggle to make God our number one priority, we should do just that. When we keep God first, it's amazing how the rest of the day—and season—will fall into place.

The whole world needs to see the jubilation we have on the inside. They need to see the difference that being one of God's children has made in us, and they need to see that, despite the turmoil of the world, we have peace in the Prince of Peace. That alone is something to smile about.

Joy to the world!

—*Connie Sturm Cameron*

Anticipation and Preparation

Dear brothers and sisters, be patient as you wait for the Lord's return. Consider the farmers who patiently wait for the rains in the fall and in the spring. They eagerly look for the valuable harvest to ripen. You, too, must be patient. Take courage, for the coming of the Lord is near.
JAMES 5:7–8

When I was a child, the month leading up to Christmas seemed interminable. The tasks to get ready were endless, from baking cookies to making and wrapping presents, to rehearsing Christmas songs, to singing in church. Christmas Eve night felt like the longest night ever, as we waited for Santa to visit our house. Once Christmas morning finally arrived, the family rule was that everyone in the house had to get up, get dressed, eat breakfast, and wash their breakfast dishes before anyone could enter the room with the tree and presents.

Unfortunately, "everyone in the house" at Christmas usually meant parents, children, grandparents, aunts, uncles, and cousins (and later a teenaged sister who didn't want to get out of bed), so this was a slow and agonizing process. Doing the required chores was more distasteful than usual, and we whined half-heartedly the entire time.

On the other hand, the long wait gave the opening of gifts even more significance.

Our hearts pounded as we finally raced to the living room and our reward!

During Advent, which means arrival or coming, we wait symbolically for the birth of Jesus. We prepare our houses, our families, and our hearts for the celebration. All our lives, too, we anticipate Christ's future return to the world, and we have God's chores to do while we wait, such as helping those in need, reading the Bible, praying, and telling others about Jesus' love. Imagine what a blessing his second coming will be after such a long wait and so much hard work. It is always Advent for Christians, so Happy Advent and Merry Christmas!

Just as we prepare for Christmas each year, we must always prepare for Christ's return to Earth.

—*Kim Sheard*

December 11
Another Name,
Another Chance

*T*he week before *Christmas*, my mother staggered downstairs wrapped in her fuzzy bathrobe. Her shoulder
bumped along the wall, and she cradled her right arm as if it
ached. I hurried to steady her.

"What's wrong?" I said. Ever the strong one, even in
crisis, she attempted to explain, but all I heard was gib-
berish.

Close friends rushed us to the emergency room where,
slumping in a wheel chair and wide-eyed as nurses bustled
around her, Mother seemed to wilt. I stroked her hair, almost
white under the harsh lights. A silver hairpin loosened,

slowly inching its way out of her hair. Then another, and another. She was coming undone, and I stifled a sob.

Before I could reposition the pins, the doctor strode in—a lanky man, all nose and legs. He touched her shoulder, then drew up a stool and eased himself down, his long hands dangling between his knees. "Hello there," he said in a kind voice. "What's your name?"

Mother chewed her lip and shifted her gaze to me. She looked scared.

"It's Helma," I said, supplying the name to which she would surely respond, but she looked at me blankly. Didn't she know who she was? Maybe she just didn't want to say it; she had always detested her name. We had heard the old story so often. Diphtheria killed the first little Helma in Mother's family of twelve, and her parents transferred the name, as well as all of her belongings, to the next baby— my mother.

"My stars," she would say, "they could have given me my own name! It's as if I was never real."

Now, the doctor flexed lean fingers around his pen and said, "Helma. That sounds Norwegian. Could you spell that for me? No? Well then, Helma, tell me what day it is."

No matter what he asked, Mother shook her head. Once, she clawed the air as if to snag an errant spider's trapeze. Then her fist dropped into her lap, furled around emptiness. It seemed like her mind's portal to language had clicked shut, locking her outside.

"Knock and the door will be opened," Jesus once said. Mother had taught me that. She'd also taught me this knocking business often involved waiting for God to answer. For the first time that day, I collected my thoughts enough to pray and beg God to heal her. Her body was what I had in mind, but God had different plans.

Shortly after she was admitted to the hospital, our pastor arrived with his King James Bible clutched in one hand. He would help us; he always had. He baptized and confirmed my three children. He helped Mother settle in with me after my husband left us. He tried hard—albeit in vain—to save my troubled brother's life. Now, he looked from Mother to me, his forehead shiny and his face crumpling.

"I've done nothing but fail you," he said, choking back a sob. "Over and over."

Dear God, did I have to comfort him, too? I stifled my frustration. "It's all right," I said and laid my hand on his shoulder. First the gesture, followed by the kindness. I felt it stirring inside, and then it was real, as if comforting him was what I had intended to do all along. Surely God was at work in this room. "You were always there, Pastor," I said. "And you're here now."

I hated leaving Mother in a strange place, scared and unable to communicate, and it felt worse when a second day passed with no change. At least she's not paralyzed, I told my kids. They wanted to know if Nana would be home

83

for presents. Would we still have Christmas? The holidays had changed drastically since my divorce, but I vowed our family traditions would continue.

Recently, I claimed their father's chair at the head of our table, the one with curved arms and a cracked spindle. I didn't really want his seat, but it looked so empty. How could I fill Mother's place, too? My faith wavered, thinning out like smoke from a chimney. Their small, worried faces renewed my resolve. "We'll celebrate," I promised. No matter what, I thought.

When I wasn't at the hospital that week, I wrapped gifts, mailed holiday cards, and baked. That's what Mother would have done. It made the awful waiting go faster, made it easier to pray—and believe—that Mother would soon answer to her unfortunate name.

On day three, she looked at me and stammered, "H-Helma. That's me. I'm Helma." I saw this as a gift from heaven, but she frowned. Was she remembering her dead sister, still resenting the secondhand name? She plucked at my sleeve as I stood to go, her eyes pleading. "H-h-home?"

My mother survived the Depression, a nervous breakdown, cancer, temporary blindness, and the loss of her hair after childbirth. She had weathered the heartache and scandal of my divorce and my brother's suicide. Daily, through it all, she had tied on a clean apron and kept the faith. She knew how to wait and trust God for a good outcome. How could I do less?

"Soon," I said and swallowed hard.

The next day, a nurse trudged in. She nodded to me briefly, plunked a red plastic tray on Mother's table, and flung open the drapes. "Mornin', Helma," she said. "How are we feeling today?" Nurse Marge's cap sat askew. She wore Reeboks and tube socks with navy stripes. Mother squinted at the tray with its four small objects.

"Honey," Marge said, "soon as you name these, Doctor said you can go on home."

Mother's eyes gleamed. "T-t-toothbrush," she said, seizing the first item and holding it to her lips.

Marge grinned and nudged her bifocals higher. She pointed again. "And these?"

Mother grabbed the pencil and scribbled on the pad of paper. I leaned closer to read it but couldn't; it was only squiggles.

"I'd say that counts," Marge said, glancing over at me. "Pencil and paper," she enunciated carefully.

Mother echoed the words, rolling them over her tongue as if tasting them. Naming is one way of hoping, they say. I bit a nail as Mother frowned at the tray. Object number four obviously baffled her.

"Never mind," I said, curling my hand around hers. "There's plenty of time to remember. Let's write your name."

Together, we spelled it out, and for a moment, I saw my mother as if she were young again. Breath held, tongue cocked between teeth, she filled her tablet with wobbly letters: *H-e-l-m-a*. "Silly name," she muttered, but she kept forming the letters.

I left her holding the tablet against her heart and watching snow flurries under the streetlight outside. What was it like to feel that the name people called you was never your own? To wait all your life for the special identity a given name confers? So many things conspire to depersonalize us. We strive to assert our true selves, to combat all the impersonal numbers assigned to us over the years—dates and statistics, grade points and salaries. Our cells and bones clock the passing time, while our souls tally decisions, dreams, and dealings of the spirit. We hunger and strive to know who we really are.

Back home, I lit the fourth *advent candle* in our wreath, hung out the vintage appliquéd felt stockings with their winking sequins, and fried the yuletide meatballs.

"How can you carry on as if nothing's wrong?" a friend asked. "You must be worried sick."

"One year, just two days before Christmas," I explained, "we buried my brother. Afterward, Mother tied on her apron and started the meatballs. All of my aunts and uncles prayed, and then we ate together. When things fall apart, my family picks up the pieces—often on our knees."

One object, yet to be named, remained on the red plastic tray. Mother could come home as soon as she could identify it. The day before Christmas, I watched her turn it over and over, her brow furrowed. I struggled to remain patient. Oh, how I longed to whisper the answer!

The time passed with no spark of recognition. She sighed and rolled over, letting the object slip from her grasp, a metallic clink against the linoleum.

"Well, what do we have here?" Marge asked, as she stooped to retrieve it.

Mother hunched her shoulders. Two hairpins worked themselves loose and skittered across the floor.

"Oh, Helma, you remember."

"I don't! And don't call me that."

Marge peered over her glasses and pursed her lips. From her pocket she pulled a block of drilled-out wood and rapped it against the table. Mother turned over, eyed it, and scowled.

"Honey, you've got to help me," Marge said, pressing the block into Mother's left palm, and the mystery object from the tray into her right hand. "I don't know how to use these. Please."

Mother was forever helping someone: a tramp, a friend, her family or neighbors. Her puzzled gaze flicked from the hollowed-out wood to the object, then back again. In the pearly light from the window, her profile glowed, a cameo. She inhaled and then slowly, tentatively, she slid the unknown object toward the block—and froze. Both arms dropped back to the blanket. Marge sighed. I sighed. She'd come so close.

A moment later, Mother looked up. "K-key," she said.

Marge let out a cheer, and my throat constricted with swallowed tears. Mother's eyes shined. Chuckling, she poked that brass key into the hole and waggled it back and forth. "I'm Helma, and this is the key."

Was there ever a happier Christmas? My children couldn't stop smiling. Mother got out her red pumps and zipped on her favorite red dress—with the green polyester slacks underneath. She twisted her hair up and pinned it securely. Then, humming "*Silver Bells*," she took her chair at our table. "Please, pass the m-m-meatballs," she said.

Mother and I celebrated twenty-five more Yuletides together. Two days shy of turning 105, she died in her sleep. By then, many awaited her final homecoming: most of her siblings, friends and neighbors, a dozen Depression-era tramps, and our pastor. Of course, there was also Daddy, my brother, Donald, and the other Helma.

I like to imagine her introducing herself to giants of the faith, like Sarah, Abraham, and Jacob. In the Old Testament, God gave those three people a new name that signified His healing transformation in their lives, a name that spoke not of their past, but their future. In my mother's case, He made a long-despised, secondhand name beautiful. Before she died, Mother shared with me the prayer she had repeated during the terrible time when she didn't know who she was. "Dear Lord, if you'll just give me back my name, I'll take care of it always. I'll love it. I promise." And Mother was as good as her word.

—*Margaret Sevenson Brendemuehl as told to Laurie Klein*

Wrapped in His Presence

For God has said, "I will never fail you. I will never
forsake you."
HEBREWS 13:5

"I want to go to the least Christmas-y place we can think of," I told my husband the year my mother died. I knew that the holidays would be hard, and I wanted to run from any reminders of past, joy-filled celebrations.

I thought if we got away from the continuous images of happy families coming home to Mom and Dad's for Christmas, we would be okay. For the first time, my husband Howard, my ten-year-old daughter Kimberly, and I would be on our own for the holidays. We would have to find new ways to enjoy this time together.

"How about Hawaii?" my husband said. We loved the islands with their pristine white-sand beaches, glittering seas, and relaxed, aloha atmosphere.

"Perfect!" I said, trying to sound enthusiastic. We could bask in the warmth of the tropical sun, swim in the pool, snorkel in the ocean, and eat fresh Mahi-Mahi and tropical fruits to our hearts' delight. We would forget all about Christmas.

The first days of our trip to the Big Island were picture-postcard perfect. We managed to leave much of our sadness behind as we reveled in the beauty of the island paradise.

Then one evening, I noticed that Howard's face was ashen, and he wasn't able to eat dinner. By morning, he was in the throes of a nasty virus, and a day later, Kimberly was ill. I was the only one who dodged the bullet, and I found myself trying to keep my emotional head above water.

On Christmas Eve, I walked a deserted beach alone. As the sun dipped low in the sky, I sank down onto the sand, tears filling my eyes. The azure sky transformed slowly into a glorious palette of pinks and scarlets, and an unexpected peace began to settle over me. God spoke to my troubled heart, "Even though you have forsaken the celebration of My Son's birth, I have not forsaken you. You can run, but never far enough to escape my loving presence. You can hide in the cave of your self-pity, but I will always seek you out. Dear one, even when you feel the most alone, I am always with you."

As sunset circled the island in silent benediction, so God's loving arms forever wrap us in His comfort and peace.

—*Susan E. Ramsden*

December 12
A Matter of Faith

When I was eight, my greatest Christmas wish was clothes for my doll. Mama had given me a real baby doll, just like the ones my friends had, but my doll came in a box with just a diaper, a small flannel sheet and a doll bottle. For Christmas, I wanted a full layette and a little baby blanket. It was deep in the heart of the Great Depression, and Mama and I lived with her parents. I had very few toys, and the baby doll was my most cherished possession, although her nakedness made me sad.

I wrote a letter to Santa and listed all the little garments I wanted for my doll. I also made sure my mother and grandmother knew what it said. So I could be even more certain, I prayed for the clothes every night, hoping that Grandma was secretly stitching them for me. After my "God bless Mama, Grandma, Grandpa, and me," I would add "Please God, my doll needs clothes and a coverlet. Will you ask Grandma to make them?" I didn't know if this was the kind of thing to put in a prayer, but I wasn't about to take any chances.

Sometimes, I heard the pedal sewing machine clicking along upstairs in Grandma's room, but if I asked her what she was making, she replied, "I'm making myself a new house dress," or, "I'm mending sheets." Grandma was dependable. She had never failed me when I made a reasonable request, but this time, I wasn't sure. Even at my young age, I knew that a layette for a doll was a luxury, and I knew Mama had no money to buy doll clothes. It had taken a long time for her to provide the doll alone.

As Christmas approached, I grew more obsessed with my desire for the doll clothes. I knew what patience was, but it applied little to me that month. I was also familiar with faith. I had heard the story of Noah and how he built the ark on faith. Grandpa had read the Christmas story in the Bible to me, so I knew it was faith that led the three Wise Men to follow the star of Bethlehem to fulfill their wish to see the new Messiah.

I had faith in Grandma and her love for me, but somehow, it wavered that December. I couldn't wait for Christmas to discover if my passionate wish would come true. There was a picture in Grandpa's Bible that showed the baby Jesus lying in a manger with only a piece of cloth underneath Him. Every time I saw the picture, I thought of my poor doll without clothes. "They both need a layette," I whispered to myself.

One morning my curiosity got the better of me, and while Grandma was noisily washing breakfast dishes and Mama was outdoors hanging laundry to dry, I sneaked up to Grandma's room. I knew I would be in big trouble if someone caught me, but I quickly and quietly peeked into drawers, boxes, and her closet to see if I could find the doll clothes I so desperately wanted.

Eventually, I found a box under some fabric. It contained an unfinished layette and a beautiful, hand-quilted coverlet just the right size for my doll. There was a fine flannel robe, embroidered with tiny flowers, a dress, a soft, knitted sweater and cap, and other items that weren't quite finished. The coverlet was a miniature quilt, pieced with what I recognized as small squares of cotton left from dresses Grandma had made for me and Mama. It was as finely worked as any of the handsome quilts on our family beds. I was breathless with excitement.

My excitement was quickly transformed to remorse for violating Grandma's privacy and her wonderful gift. Suddenly, I felt the pain she would feel if she knew I had spoiled her surprise. In addition, I had disappointed myself, because now I would have to pretend on Christmas morning. My guilt grew as I thought about the pretense to come.

Early Christmas morning, I heard Grandpa going downstairs to light the gas heaters and start the breakfast coffee. Usually, I rushed to be with him, but that year, I laid very still in my bed. My regret over having ruined Grandma's surprise, even if she didn't know, almost overshadowed my joy at knowing I would at last have lovely clothes for my doll. I vowed I would never be so untrustworthy and lacking in faith again. I asked God to be strong and to never disappoint myself or anyone again. At last, Grandpa came upstairs. He tossed my Christmas stocking onto my bed and called out, "Merry Christmas, everybody! Time to get up."

I was thrilled with my doll's new clothes and coverlet, and no one guessed how hard it was for me not to reveal my guilty secret. At least, that was my hope. I unwrapped each tiny garment and laid it out for the family to see. Each one was stitched so exquisitely and so perfectly from Grandma's loving hands. No one else could make such tiny stitches. I tried each piece on my doll, and when she was dressed, I believed she was the most beautiful doll in the world.

Grandpa brought out a wicker doll buggy for her, just like the one my mother had used for me when I was an infant. I put my doll in it and tucked her in with the precious quilt and pillow. My joy was complete, and I burst into tears. Looking back, I think that may have been the first time in my life that I cried from happiness. I never doubted my Grandma again. Like God, she provided the

95

things I desired, as long as it was good for me. Her gifts, as well as those from the Lord, would always exceed my expectations because they were given with love.

I have often longed for the magic of the season to do its work in my life. I've prayed for the peace and faith that represent the real meaning of Christmas—the celebration of Christ's coming to Earth to live and die for each of us who believe. How many times in my seventy-odd years have I had to curb my patience with the way things are on this Earth? How many times have I needed to remind myself that faith is a gift from God? Faith is simple, yet so difficult sometimes for us humans. On that Christmas so many years ago, God reminded me that life's lessons, no matter how difficult, strengthen our struggling faith.

—*Marcia E. Brown*

A Piece of Straw

Create in me a clean heart, O God,
Renew a loyal Spirit within me.
PSALM 51:10

I discovered it a few days after Christmas. Tucked in the crack between the carpet and wall, I found a slender piece of straw. The Christmas decorations had been packed and carried to the attic. All evidence of Christmas had been stored away until next year. Christmas was over.

My mind had already moved to other thoughts. In my haste to get the house in order, I had missed this one sprig of wheat-colored straw. This fragment of straw had been spread with others of its kind around the crèche that adorned our mantel during the Christmas holiday.

Years before, the nativity scene had looked stark when our family placed the figures of Mary, Joseph, and the baby Jesus on the mantel. "The crèche needs some straw," I said. Our youngest son accepted the task and darted out the door. He returned from his hunt grasping a large cluster of straw in his hand. Where he found straw in our suburban area has remained his secret.

We sprinkled the strands of straw around the Holy Family crouched in their rustic shed. We filled the manger as we imagined it being over 2,000 years ago in a simple stable. The straw enhanced the figures and made the scene more lifelike. Each year we saved the same worn shards and tucked them around the Christ child as reverently as Mary would have wrapped the babe in swaddling cloths.

I stared at the single piece of straw in my hand. The memory of our Christmas ritual jarred my spirit that had already begun a journey toward forgetfulness. Without realizing it, I had allowed the message of Christmas to dim along with the removal of the colored lights and extinguished candles.

The Lord often startles us with the unexpected. Incredibly, a simple strand of straw jolted me to remember the miracle of Christ's birth. Christmas is never over. The Christmas season lasts as long as Christ lives in our hearts.

Let the joy of Christmas live on throughout the year.

—*Barbara Brady*

December 13
The Gypsy

Like most winter days in England, the sky was tinged with the promise of rain to come. Tucked away in a chilly corner bedroom and surrounded by stacks of books, I tried my best to study for my upcoming tutorial session at Oxford. My eyes blurred as I scanned each page, and with Christmas just around the corner, my heart ached for home. With a sigh, I picked up my poetry once more.

Thunk! The sound of the mail sliding in the door slot saved me from my drudgery. With a hopeful heart I flew downstairs and flipped through the small stack of mail. There was a package for me! I ripped the brown paper as quickly as I could. A tape fell out of the box, along with a note from my college boyfriend. "Here are some of my favorite songs," my future husband wrote. "I hope they encourage you as much as they do me."

I popped the tape into my personal music player, and listened hungrily to the songs from home. The music he had chosen lifted my spirits and challenged my heart. With a haunting refrain, one chorus pierced deep into my soul. "I'll give, and I'll hold nothing. I'll give and I'll hold nothing. I'll give and I'll hold nothing back."

Tears slipped down my cheeks. In the quiet of my house, I sang along at the top of my lungs. Lord, I'm just a poor college student, I prayed. I don't really have anything to give, but if I have something I can give, I will. I will hold nothing back.

As if on cue, there was another sound at the door. Who could it be? As American students far from home, my flat mates and I didn't have many visitors, especially not during study hours. Curious, I turned off my music and thumped down the creaky Victorian stairs once more. I unlatched the door and peered through the crack. My heart sank when I saw the Gypsy woman.

Her dark, bright eyes were young, but her weather-worn face was creased with worry. She had a nose ring and wore a brightly colored scarf around her head. She jostled a small baby—no more than two—on her hip, his nose running from the cold.

"Can I help you?" I asked, dreading the answer. I had been warned that Gypsies were homeless nomads, some of them known to survive on begging and pickpocketing. Maybe her husband is sending her door to door and using the baby to make money, I thought as I remembered the stories I had heard. Even if I had any money—which I didn't—I certainly wouldn't give it to her.

"My baby is sick," the Gypsy mother said in a pitiful voice. "Could you spare some change for the doctor?"

Firmly resolved, I shook my head. "I'm sorry," I replied. "I'm just a student. I don't have much of anything." Just then, the words of the song and my promised prayer flashed into my head. I'll give and I'll hold nothing back.

I knew that no coincidence had brought her to my door, just as God had spoken to me through the words of that song. "Wait here." I sighed. "I'll be right back."

What could I possibly give her? I really didn't have any money. As I moved toward the kitchen, I suddenly had an idea. If I couldn't give her money, the very least I could do was give her something to eat for herself and the baby. I scanned the room for some food I could spare. I didn't really need those chocolate popsicles. There was a fresh loaf of bread in case she wanted to make sandwiches, and a can of soup.

Food in hand, my jaded heart opened up with a pulse of generosity. "Here!" I said, opening the door and shoving the soup and bread into the young mother's free arm. "I don't have any money to give you, but I do have this. I got you popsicles, too—just for fun."

Nose still running, the baby greedily sucked the Popsicle, even with the frosty chill in the air. The weary mother thanked me, took the food, and silently walked away.

"God bless you!" I called and softly shut the door.

As I pondered this odd turn of events, something still didn't feel quite right. The face of the hungry woman and child burned in my mind. The song's call—and my promise—echoed in my heart. I'll give and I'll hold nothing back. In that instant, it all became clear. I had more to give! I rushed to gather even more of my freshly purchased groceries into plastic bags. I have two boxes of cereal; maybe, I could give her one, and my extra gallon of milk for the baby.

Groceries in hand, I ran out the door, and out into the lane. Legs churning, I chased down the disappearing pair. "Wait!" I called out. "I have more."

The brightly colored figure stopped and turned to face me. "Here is some more food for you, and some milk for the baby," I said.

She nodded and took the food. "Thank you," she said simply and continued on her way.

I jogged back home and collapsed into a chair beside my kitchen table to rest. As I gazed around the room, the

magnitude of what I had just done began to sink in. The

shelves were nearly empty. The food on top of the refrigerator was gone. True to my promise, I had held nothing back, and now I had nothing to eat.

My stomach rumbled, and my eyes darted once more to the empty pantry. I'm glad I gave it away, Lord. I want to sacrifice, like you did for me, but did I really have to give all of it away? A tear of regret trickled down my cheek. I really needed that can of soup and the bread. What would I do now? I looked at the clock. It was time to go to the library for more studying. I packed up my books, donned my raincoat, and headed out into the cold.

Even this close to Christmas, the roses in the English gardens were fully in bloom. Their soft petals thriving in the bitter cold gave me hope. "Lord," I prayed, "if you can provide for a Christmas rose, I trust that you can provide for me."

I rounded the corner, and there, sitting out on top of the brick garden wall, was the most amazing sight: my can of soup and my loaf of bread.

The Gypsy woman had left behind the very items I desperately needed to feed myself. I had held nothing back, and neither had my Heavenly Father.

So far from home for the holidays, God had met me in my loneliness through the unexpected gift of music. He challenged the boundaries of my generosity through a hungry Gypsy mother and her child. As I placed my trust in

Him, He provided for my most specific needs and prepared me for a lifetime of dependence on His generous love.

That blustery winter day, a wandering Gypsy woman and her child taught me a lesson that an innkeeper in Bethlehem learned more than 2,000 years ago. Give and hold nothing back. You just might receive the greatest gift of all.

—*Katherine Ryan Craddock*

Crowding Jesus

*Even the sparrow finds a home, and the swallow builds her
nest and raises her young at a place near your altar, O Lord
of Heaven's armies, my King and my God!*
PSALM 84:3

Early in our marriage, my husband brought a beautiful
hand-carved Nativity set home from a trip to Ecuador. It
became our tradition to arrange the lovely wooden figures on a spotless white tablecloth. We placed Baby Jesus
in the center with the other characters grouped carefully
around him, each one standing or kneeling at a respect-
ful distance. I thought it looked perfect.

Things changed after our two children were born.
When they were old enough, they took the job of setting
up the Nativity set upon themselves. It wasn't long before
the set suffered some wear and tear. Each year, they reverently unwrapped and exclaimed over each figure: the angel
with the missing wing, the beautiful donkey with its kind
expression, the impossibly tall Wise Men with their mysterious gifts, and, best of all, Baby Jesus whose right foot had
been eaten by the dog.

With no sense of placement or spacing, they crowded
all the figures, including the donkey, around the manger,

each one as close to Jesus as possible. No matter how many times I spread the figures into a more pleasing tableau, the next time I looked, they all would be squashed up against each other and grouped around the manger in one large clump—much like eager children who just want to see and be close.

As I came upon the scene one day, I realized how closely it resembled God's desire for His children. He has always wanted us to be as close to Jesus as we can, regardless of how it may look to others. Our focus ought to be on Him as the center of our world, and we should be eager to see Him above all else. That's when I understood that this was what I wanted for my children, as well. I wanted to raise them in the peace and joy of the Lord's constant presence and to make our home next to His altar, where we can spend our days gazing at Him in wonder and adoration. I gave the Nativity set one more look, and I decided it was perfect—just the way it was.

We belong right next to Jesus.

—*Becky Fulcher*

December 14
I Can Give Him My Heart

In the bleak mid-winter

Frosty wind made moan,

"Nothing in there that you want," I said to my dog, who was sniffing eagerly at the pile of boxes. "Maybe nothing I want either," I added to myself. The sky was gray; the wind blew around the corners of the house. I felt none of the excitement that had always characterized the days after Thanksgiving. None of the eagerness to decorate that had led my family to coin the term, "Christmas-tree-putting-up."

I got out my old Nativity scene, complete with the baby snuggled in a bed of pine needles from previous Christmases, and began to set the figures on a shelf. As a child, I had supplemented the scene with my dollhouse people. "Now, Susie can sit here by the baby's mommy," I would say as I moved them to the stable. "Tommy can climb on the roof by the angel. I'll put the dogs over here and give the baby a puppy to play with." My father had labeled the box "CRESH" in black marker, and every year we laughed at his spelling error.

This was the first time I had opened the boxes since putting everything away last Christmas, less than a month before my father's death. Every year since I left home, I had faithfully driven back to St. Louis to spend Christmas with my parents. Every year, I carefully decorated the house in our traditional way: bird on the lamp, balls on the stair railing, crèche on the end table, village scene on the tree skirt, beavers on the mantel, and the train around the tree.

Maybe this is what it feels like to be pruned, I thought. People had died or moved away. Some just walked out of my life; others had made different plans. "No one's left," I said to myself, looking around the room.

Earth stood hard as iron,

Water like a stone;

"It's too hard!" I said, more to hear my own voice than to communicate. "It's as if my heart's frozen. I'm all alone for Christmas, and I don't know what to do." I sat down amid the clutter of decorations and pressed my fingertips against my eyes to hold back the tears. If this were a story, I told myself, I would bravely seek out other lonely people and give them a happy Christmas, thereby making one for myself. I rested my head on the sofa arm to hide the tears I could no longer restrain.

Snow had fallen, snow on snow,

Snow on snow,
In the bleak mid-winter,
Long ago.

"Want to help me decorate my Christmas tree?" I said to a friend. "I've got it set up already, but I'd love company for the decorating part."

Later, I took the string of lights from her and said, "That's not how it goes. You have to start at the bottom, and zigzag."

"What? How come?" Cheryl asked, laughing.

"That's how my father taught me to do it," I explained, clipping the lights to the branches. "You use the wires to help hold the branches up, and you spiral around the tree. According to my father, we couldn't have two bulbs the same color next to each other, either." I sat back on my heels to rest my back a moment.

"It must be hard," Cheryl said, "being alone at Christmas for the first time."

"Oh, not really," I said. "I've got friends, you know."

We hung ornaments quietly for a few minutes. Then, I lifted a felt tree with sequins and said, "We made these in Brownies. Mother always said she couldn't believe how many tangles a group of little girls could make in one piece of thread. We bought those glass balls from Ann, a neighbor girl. The candle came from my grandmother's childhood tree. Mother collected beavers, so we've got a lot of them."

The wind rattled sleet against the window, startling us both. "Yes, it's hard, being alone this Christmas," I admitted.

"I know I'm not really alone. I do have friends, and there's always Jesus, but I still feel pretty desolate sometimes." I picked up another box of ornaments.

Our God, heaven cannot hold Him

Nor earth sustain ...
Heaven and earth shall flee away
When He comes to reign.

"Joy to the world!" I shifted from alto to tenor to fill out the chord. The lights had been dimmed, and at the end of the service, the congregation would "pass the light" until everyone held a lighted candle. I tried the descant to "Oh Come All Ye Faithful," but the children in front of me turned around to stare. It didn't sound as good an octave lower anyway, I thought.

I loved the old carols. The family had always gone to the choir program at the high school, even after I graduated. Every year the neighborhood had gone caroling up and down the street. There were so many participants that my parents would invite Granny over so someone would be home to hear the carols. Afterward, we gathered at someone's house for cider, brownies, and cookies.

After my mother became too disabled to go out caroling, the neighborhood had switched to just having the party, singing by the fireplace while sharing Christmas goodies. Usually, I brought my guitar for accompaniment. I taught the children the motions to "Away in a Manger."

Most of the neighborhood kids weren't sure what the song was about, so I often told the old story. I also did the silly line-endings in "Rudolph," and the kids were always surprised to find an adult who would join them in chanting, "like a light bulb!"

"Silent night, holy night!" the congregation sang. I didn't attempt the counterpart.

> *In the bleak mid-winter, a stable place sufficed*
> *The Lord God Almighty, Jesus Christ.*

On Christmas morning, I drove the icy streets slowly, enjoying the lights punctuating the darkness. I could see the brilliance of my friends' house from blocks away. This isn't how Christmas morning is supposed to be, I thought. I should be home, heating water for tea and tucking treats into the dog's stocking, hung on the mantel with the rest. We would eat the traditional cinnamon rolls and open our stockings before sorting out the presents. One at a time, around the room, we would open the gifts, exclaiming and laughing at the tags, trying things on, occasionally getting up to let the dog out or check the game hens baking for dinner.

I parked in front of my friends' house and carried my boxes in, emptying them under the tree. I couldn't help but notice that the light strings weren't holding the branches up.

"Elsi's here!" Jo said. "Okay, Matthew you can come in now."

Matthew scampered into the living room to find his Santa present, an enormous Lego kit sitting unwrapped in front of the tree.

"Want some cocoa?" Jo offered. "Why don't you sit over here?"

Gratefully, I tucked myself into the chair. The stockings, including mine, were leaning on the windowsill, not hanging from a mantel. They wouldn't be opened until the gifts were finished and everyone had had breakfast. Everything's so different, I told myself. Then, I added sternly, Now, stop that!

Paul put on his Santa hat and started to hand out gifts. I didn't know my eyes were filled with tears until the tree lights began to blur.

Angels and archangels may have gathered there;
Cherubim and seraphim thronged the air.

This is your birthday, Lord, I prayed silently. It's not supposed to be about me and what I want. It's about you, who you are and what you do. I miss all the old, familiar traditions and people, Abba. Father, help me remember what really matters.

But His mother only, in her maiden bliss,
Worshiped the beloved with a kiss.

"Here's one for you, Elsi!" I blinked away my tears and took the small package. I read the tag, "To Elsi From Matthew."

"Oh, a turtle bookmark," I said. "Thanks!"

The little boy looked up at me. "Jo told me you like to read, and you like turtles. I spent my own money on it. Is it a good present?"

At that moment, it finally felt like Christmas. "It's not only a good present," I told him. "It is absolutely the right present. Merry Christmas!" I looked around, and my focus shifted.

The people here weren't my family, and my traditions were nowhere to be found. Yet, the room and my heart were filled with the joy and love of Christmas. Suddenly, I realized I was humming the last verse of Christina Rosetti's poem.

What can I give Him,

Old as I am?
If I were a shepherd
I would bring a lamb;
If I were a wise man
I would do my part;
What can I give him?
Give Him my heart!

—*Elsi Dodge*

A Precious Name

And she will have a son, and you are to name him Jesus, for
he will save his people from their sins.
MATTHEW 1:21

I shifted restlessly on the wooden pew, my hands resting on my swollen belly. The church was dark save a lone spotlight shining on the stage to highlight the nativity scene. I watched the familiar story unfold. Mary's condition resonated with me, since I was seven months pregnant with my second child. A bumpy, dusty ride on a donkey sounded miserable and would definitely induce labor, I reflected soberly.

My husband and I had recently separated, and I didn't know if I was going to be raising this new baby by myself. The thought terrified me. For now, I relaxed and enjoyed the Christmas pageant and chose not to worry about an uncertain future.

I had been pondering baby names. I had a girl's name selected, but I couldn't settle on a boy's name. I liked Jeffrey Alan, but I wasn't certain. Mary and Joseph didn't face that dilemma; the angel had instructed them, "And you shall call his name, Jesus." What about my unborn child? I wanted some angelic direction as well. Choosing a suitable name was a formidable challenge.

As I continued watching the pageant, I gained a new perspective on the age-old story. I had always focused on Mary and the infant Jesus, but now I wondered about Joseph. What kind of man was he? He had a pregnant wife, and he wasn't the father of the unborn child. Undoubtedly, he endured rumors and mocking, but after receiving a dream from God, he was obedient to God's will.

The Bible describes him as a righteous man. He raised Jesus as his own son and taught him carpentry—the family business. He was a man who listened to God, obeyed Him, and he obviously loved his wife and family. I had never really thought about it before.

My own baby boy was born on January 29, and I named him Joseph Andrew. I prayed he would grow to be a man who listens to God and obeys His will. As it turned out, I received some angelic direction that Christmas, after all.

God knew our names before we were born.

—*Connie Hilton Dunn*

December 15
Russian Tarts

When I married a man with eight brothers and sisters, the term family dinner took on a whole new meaning. I watched in astonishment as herds of people gathered to eat enough food to feed our immediate family of seven for a week.

Trepidation replaced amazement as I realized that someday it would be my turn to host the horde. The opportunity arrived when one of my sisters-in-law announced at Thanksgiving that everyone would be thrilled to come to our place for Christmas dinner. "You don't want to load all the children into the car and go anywhere on Christmas Day," she said. "And I'm sure they'd much rather stay home and play with all their new toys and gifts."

I smiled and said, "Of course. We'd love to."

When Tom and I were finally alone, I revealed my terrible secret. "I've never cooked Christmas dinner," I said.

His eyes widened as though I'd just confessed to a bank robbery. "You're kidding. How did that happen?"

"Well, my mother insisted on cooking it every year, and after she died, we always had dinner with one of my relatives."

"You'll be fine. I'll help you. After all, how hard can it be?"

He's right, I thought. I remembered the countless dinners my mother had organized, prepared, and served. She made it all look easy and enjoyable. Without realizing it, I had learned a lot. I doubted I could fill her shoes, but I could definitely try them on.

I immediately started to think about the menu. I'll make Russian tarts, I decided. My mother had made them every year, just as her mother had. They were my family's definitive Christmas treat. I would carry on the tradition and share it with my new family.

I planned a simple and manageable dinner, but like Mickey Mouse in "The Sorcerer's Apprentice," the scene took on a nightmarish quality as more and more food arrived from the kitchen. Every time I lowered myself into my chair, someone asked me for something that was missing, or I thought of an item I'd forgotten. I wondered if I stopped trying to sit down, the spell would be broken and the dishes would cease their nauseating march through the swinging door. Relax, I thought. Like a visit to the dentist or childbirth, it had to end eventually.

After dinner, an obscene amount of food was carried back to the kitchen. Our dog, Nick, looked up at me as if to say, "Just scrape it on the floor. I'll take care of it, and I'll never tell."

"Sorry, Nick," I said, and began to put the leftovers into countless little plastic containers. Plates and cutlery went into the dishwasher. Pots and pans that wouldn't fit, or ones too crusted with mashed potatoes or other unidentifiable substances to come clean, littered the counters. I took a deep breath, donned my yellow rubber gloves, and began to run the hot water.

I gazed out the kitchen window, suddenly filled with the terrible ache of missing my mother. "I wish you could have been here," I whispered. Tears filled my eyes. I had tried so hard to make Christmas special, just as she had always done, but something had gone wrong. And then my oldest son appeared and picked up a towel. "Can I help?" he asked. He couldn't dry dishes to save his life, and I kept tripping over his size-fifteen feet, but as I watched him work, I was reminded once again of how incredibly lucky I was to have a loving husband, five remarkable children, and a life filled with countless blessings.

That was when I realized why Christmas with my mother had always been so magical. As a tribute to God's greatest gift, she transformed everything she did for Christmas into a celebration of the miraculous. And just like me, she had been surrounded by miracles. Breaking my reverie, Tom came up behind me and put his arms around my waist. "You were amazing today," he said. "I'm so proud of you."

I relished the feeling of satisfaction that spread through me. I did it, I thought. I cooked Christmas dinner. "You know what?" I said. "I'm glad your sister asked us to have Christmas dinner."

"Really? It was pretty chaotic and it was so much work for you. You didn't even get a chance to eat."

"Yeah, but I think everybody had a nice time, and I know the kids enjoyed spending the whole day here. I couldn't have done it without you," I said and kissed him.

"Or my mom."

"Your mom?"

"You bet," I said and smiled. Mom had been here, alive in the years of memories she created for my brother and me, memories that gave birth to the traditions I now shared with her grandchildren. She had been right beside me all day long, coaching me through my first Christmas dinner. And when had I needed her most, God sent her grandson into the kitchen to give me a refresher course on miracles.

I went into the dining room. A plate of Russian tarts sat on the table. Suddenly hungry, I picked one up and bit into it. Not bad, I thought. Not bad at all.

—*Susan B. Townsend*

The Homecoming

There is more than enough room in my Father's home. If this were not so, would I have told you that I am going to prepare a place for you?
JOHN 14:2

Mother was a very private person who never shared her beliefs about living or dying. However, her participation in manifold church activities was an inspiration to me and a testament to her deep Christian roots.

After our marriage, my husband and I moved to the city where his family lived. Each Christmas my parents joined us. Mother played the piano as we sang our favorite carols and hymns. My mother-in-law made delicious candy and other tempting dishes. We celebrated the birth of Jesus and praised Him for the blessings he bestowed on our family.

Mother's last Christmas was spent in the hospital undergoing treatments for pancreatic cancer. Dad, my husband and I, our three children, Mother's brother, and my mother-in-law shared a suite at the Hilton. A small green ceramic tree with multicolored lights sat on a table surrounded by gaily wrapped packages.

We tried to maintain a happy mood, especially for Dad, who appeared to be in denial. After Mother's operation in May, we had all heard the surgeon when he gave her two months to live, but it seemed that Dad had chosen to ignore the doctor's prognosis. We had only two months left, and I had so many unanswered questions. We lived in different cities, and Dad always answered the phone. We never talked about Mother's feelings. Obviously, she intended to protect him from the truth.

So, there we were with the tree lights glowing, Christmas candy in a dish, and the words to carols stuck in my throat. A basket filled with small gifts wrapped in ironed white tissue paper caught my attention. Mother recycled everything. She had selected items from home she hoped would have meaning for each of us: a porcelain man and woman for me and a crystal duck for our youngest son. Her actions of love spoke volumes for the real words she found so difficult to express. Months later, Mother went into a coma mid-morning, but just after midnight, she lifted herself up, opened her eyes, and said, "Oh, it's Jesus." She lay back against the pillows and passed away about an hour later.

For thirty years, that ceramic Christmas tree has glowed in my home during the month of December. It stands as a reminder of the night my mother went to be with her Lord—but not before she answered all my questions.

Miracles happen when we least expect them.

—*Beth Lynn Clegg*

December 16
An Old-Fashioned Christmas

I sat at my desk stunned by the news I just received. "We are eliminating your position effective today," my boss of only three months informed me. "You have two hours to pack your personal belongings and leave."

He reviewed the terms of my separation agreement, but I heard little. As a human resources manager, I was all too familiar with the legalese contained in a separation agreement because I had reviewed it many times before with employees whose positions were eliminated long before my own.

His voice faded into the background, while my thoughts continued to scatter. How would I pay the mortgage? How would I feed my kids? Where was I going to find health insurance for us? How could he do this right before Christmas? I'm a single mom. What am I going to do? "Do you have any questions?" he asked, interrupting my worries.

"No, no questions," I replied. "I know the routine."

For the next two hours, I packed my career into storage boxes. Employees who learned of the position elimination stopped at my office to share a hug, cry with me, provide personal contact information, and to wish me well. At the end of the two hours, I left behind an extremely stressful job. My only fear was what lay ahead.

With Christmas just a few weeks away and a small severance package provided, I took advantage of the paid time off to finish up Christmas-related errands.

Several weeks earlier, I had been asked to share "What an old-fashioned Christmas means to me" with my church's small study group the Sunday following my Friday layoff. After spending the better part of Saturday contemplating what I would share, I logged onto my computer and worked well into the night.

That Sunday, as I walked to the podium to speak, I asked God to give me the emotional strength to deliver the teaching in its entirety. I swallowed hard and I began. "When we look at the individuals in the Christmas story as found in Matthew chapter two, we can't help but see that the people who were integral to the story were just like you and me. They had choices to make.

"First, there was Mary. Only a teenager at the time, Mary was told she would give birth to the Messiah. She could have said, 'No way, God, get someone else.' God knew Mary would be obedient. Mary chose to trust God. She probably saw firsthand the many times God had been faithful to the Jews, providing for their needs. Even to the point of possibly being stoned to death for being falsely accused of adultery, Mary still chose to trust God."

I scanned the faces in front of me and struggled to remain calm in order to deliver my message. I began to speak again, more slowly this time as my nerves steadied. "Then there was Joseph. The Bible tells us he was a righteous man, and like Mary, he had been chosen to raise Jesus and teach Him the laws and practices of the Jewish people. When Joseph was told to take Mary as his wife, he could have said, 'No way! I'm out of here.' Instead, he also chose to trust the Lord."

I swallowed hard. I knew what was coming next, and I could feel a lump in my throat beginning to form. I took a deep breath and held on tightly to the sides of the podium. "None of you know this because I haven't shared this news with anyone. This past Friday, my position with my company was eliminated. Today I have a choice to make.

"What am I giving to God this Christmas? I've chosen to give Him my trust and my obedience. I will trust that He knows my financial situation and will provide for my needs. I will obey His command to 'fear not.'

"Trust doesn't mean I will sit back, do nothing, and wait for a job offer. I have to do my part while God does His.

Because I've been laid off, I'll be unable to give my family and friends the usual, extravagant Christmas with an abundance of presents as I've done in the past." I felt tears of self-pity pricking my eyes, but I paused for a moment and shrugged them off.

When I continued, I told my audience how I researched the history of Christmas celebrations and how I tried to find the true definition of an old-fashioned Christmas. "I discovered it had nothing to do with extravagance. As I read through century-old diaries I found on the Internet, I looked at the entries written close to Christmas. People didn't have significant amounts of money to spend on store-bought gifts, so in many cases gifts were handmade: a special handmade card, a paper bookmark, a lock of hair braided and tied with a bit of beautiful ribbon."

I talked about other gifts I found recorded in the old diaries, as well as the entries that spoke of how grateful the recipients were for the sacrifice of time and talent. However, the warmest memories the diarists wrote about were the ones involving time spent around the fireplace sharing a Christmas song, a story, and heartfelt love.

"God doesn't want material things; God wants you," I said. "So, what will you give God this Christmas? Your time? Your talents? Your heart and your life? I have chosen to trust God and give Him my future, my career, and my abilities and allow Him to use them in the manner He decides. As the Magi laid down their gifts before Jesus, I encourage you lay down whatever it is that God is asking you to give Him. He will take what you give Him and use it to bless others, and when God uses you in that manner, it is the greatest gift of all."

I closed my notebook and stepped away from the podium. No one spoke. When Pastor Tom joined me at the podium, he didn't speak either. After a few moments of silence, he took the microphone in his hand, hesitated, and then said quietly, "Wow, what a powerful message."

Judging by similar responses I heard later, it was evident the message hit home to many, which was an answer to my prayer.

As Christmas drew closer I experienced a peace and tranquility in my life such as I had never experienced. Christmas took on a new, more sacred meaning. The business of "getting it all done" was replaced with a relaxed pace and a renewed appreciation of the reason for the season.

My children delighted in the few gifts I was able to provide, but they expressed a preference for simply gathering around the dinner table with family.

Shortly after Christmas, while searching the Internet for a new position, I came across a job title that sounded intriguing: life coach. I clicked on the link and read about the opportunity to help people dream big and go after the job of their dreams. Helping others to achieve their lifelong dream had always been my dream, but I never knew it was possible to do it and get paid at the same time.

As I dialed the phone to obtain further information about the job, I thought about the blessing of being laid off. God needed to get my attention, and with the stress and fast pace of my former job, He knew I wouldn't take the time to listen. He wanted to teach me firsthand about trust, just as He had taught Mary and Joseph. When I chose to trust, God gave me the greatest gift I had ever received—the peace, tranquility, and joy of an old-fashioned Christmas.

—Elisa Yager

Christmas Bears

*You must each decide in your heart how much to give. And
don't give reluctantly or in response to pressure. For God
loves a person who gives cheerfully.*
2 CORINTHIANS 9:7

I stood in line at the checkout counter while the cashier
took care of the customer in front of me. As my Christmas bows and gift tags moved along the conveyor belt,
I calculated how much they would cost. I counted my
money, and with a great sense of relief, I realized I had
just enough cash to pay for them without resorting to my
debit card.

The cashier finished ringing up my items. Then, she
pointed to an arrangement of stuffed bears in a variety of
sizes and colors at the end of the counter, all staring at me
with dark, plastic eyes. "Would you like to donate a teddy
bear to the Children's Hospital?"

I almost said, "Not today. I have only enough for these
items." Still, the thought of a sick child tugged at my heart.
A long time ago, my seven-year-old brother died in a hospital, and I would have done anything to ease his pain.
"Sure, I'll pay for a bear," I said and dug into my purse for
my debit card.

"Do you want to pick one out?" the cashier asked.

I was in a hurry. "Any one of them is fine," I said. Then I noticed that some looked nicer than others. I reached for a medium-sized brown bear with a pink bow tied around his neck. His fur was surprisingly soft. I handed him to the cashier, and she scanned the tag sticking out of his side.

"Thank you," she said and gave him back to me along with my bag of items. "There's a bin for the bears over there."

I turned and was surprised to see a waist high bin filled almost to the top with teddy bears. I felt a little ashamed by my hesitation to buy one, when so many other shoppers had opened their hearts and their wallets. Somehow, as I found myself caught up in the commercial aspect of Christmas, I had forgotten the real meaning of the season. I dropped my bear into the bin and imagined the smile on the face of the child who would receive it.

When we get caught up in earthly worries, we sometimes forget the needs of others.

—Mary Laufer

December 17
Michael's Message

had made my decision. I wasn't going to indulge in a pity party for myself just because my children weren't coming home for Christmas. Since the true spirit of Christmas focuses upon others, I turned down all dinner invitations and planned my strategy. I would prepare turkey dinners with all the trimmings for others less fortunate. I love to cook and relish experimenting with gourmet dishes. When I'm not at my computer, my kitchen is turned upside-down while I prepare a few favorite dishes.

One of my tastiest concoctions was bread filling, and for years, my stuffed turkeys had been in demand by my family. This Christmas, however, I would adopt new families and attempt to relieve someone's loneliness. I decided to start by offering to prepare a turkey dinner for the residents of a mental health unit where I used to work. Then I planned to do likewise for the elderly residents in a personal care boarding home nearby.

Christmas day arrived. I awoke early and imagined the bubbling excitement of my grandchildren opening their presents, but I shook off my sadness and renewed my determination to make the best of it. Sure enough, my busy kitchen clutter helped erase the pain of my family's absence. When the first meal was prepared, I put the second smaller turkey in the oven. It would roast while I served the twelve men at the mental health unit.

At my first stop, I couldn't help but notice one man's misguided attempt to prepare dinner. He had shoved a whole turkey, giblets and all, into a kettle filled to the brim with rapidly boiling water. I was excited by the prospect of serving him a real Christmas dinner. A thrill passed through me when the eyes of all twelve men opened wide as they sat down to a table decked with a golden-browned turkey, well-seasoned stuffing, creamy whipped potatoes, giblet gravy, colorful vegetables, cranberry sauce, and every imaginable condiment. After bowing their heads in thanksgiving, they piled their plates high with turkey and all the trimmings. We laughed as one by one they loosened their belts to make room for the pumpkin pie.

Later, I loaded my nearly emptied pans into the trunk of the car. The men had devoured all but enough for one or two meals. They waved and called out to me when I pulled out of my parking space and drove to the corner of the alley. As I put on the brakes, I noticed a huge, red-bearded man, wearing a ragged black coat and knitted skullcap, seated on a concrete step. He was rummaging through a knapsack, but he looked up as the car pulled to a stop beside him.

His blue eyes met mine, and something turned over inside me. On an impulse, I turned off the ignition and got out of the car. "Merry Christmas," I said before I realized the absurdity of my greeting in light of his apparent circumstances.

"Merry Christmas to you, Ma'am," he responded politely, shielding his eyes from the sun's rays.

Embarrassed, I hesitated. Talking to strange men in alleys wasn't a habit of mine, yet something about this stranger captivated me. Although his clothing was ragged, he looked clean. His bluer than blue eyes crinkled bright and clear, and he appeared sober.

"I don't mean to be nosy, but have you had Christmas dinner today?" I asked.

"No, Ma'am," he replied. "I'm just passing through. I left Connecticut yesterday trying to get to a warmer climate, farther south. I guess this is pretty warm for Pennsylvania. Sure glad it's not snowing," he added and looked up at the sky. I considered the leftovers in the trunk, but the stranger interrupted my thoughts. "My name is Michael," he said with a grin.

"Glad to meet you, Michael. I'm Penny." I could give him those leftovers, I decided, but I have another turkey to carve; it should be about ready. Besides, I have no plate or silverware. Then I remembered Bethesda Mission. "There's a mission right around the corner, Michael. They're serving dinners today. You could even get a bed for the night."

"Thank you, Ma'am. I'll keep that in mind." His blue eyes studied me.

Somehow, I couldn't leave. "I'm going that way. I'd be glad to drop you off," I said and seriously questioned my sanity for offering a stranger a ride.

"That's all right, ma'am. I'm sure I can find it. Thank you, anyhow."

Thoughts of the leftovers continued to nag me. Oh well, I thought, he probably wouldn't accept them. "Michael, I have to go now, but if you need anything, I'm sure the mission will help." Then, with one last feeble effort to do my Christian duty, I said, "I don't know anything about you, but I want you to know God loves you and I'll be praying for you."

"Thank you, ma'am. May God bless you."

I fumbled with the ring of keys in my hand. "Merry Christmas to you. It was nice talking to you," I said. For some reason, I felt flustered. As I drove off, the nagging I had felt returned in the form of scripture. "Suppose you see a brother or sister who has no food or clothing, and you say, 'Good-bye and have a good day; stay warm and eat well'—but then you don't give that person any food or clothing. What good does that do?" (James 2:15–16).

How could I have driven off, food in the trunk, and left him there? What was wrong with me? I whipped the car around the block and skidded to a stop at the corner, but the stranger was gone. He couldn't be far, I reasoned. I'd only been a few minutes. Desperately, I searched the deserted streets. Perhaps he had taken my advice after all. I drove toward the mission, peering in doorways along the way. I went around in circles, searching alleys and every street leading off from the corner of the alley. Michael had seemingly vanished.

Disappointed, I finally headed for home. My Christmas dinner for twelve had surely been intended for thirteen—now, I was certain. As I drove home, reflecting upon the events of the day, I realized that my efforts to relieve my loneliness might have interfered with a divine appointment. I should have been more sensitive to the unplanned opportunity that crossed my path. I resolved that if a similar occasion should ever present itself, I would follow my heart rather than my head. After all, I may have missed the honor of sharing a meal with an angel.

—*Penny Smith*

Making a Difference

All must give as they are able, according to the blessings
given to them by the Lord your God.
DEUTERONOMY 16:17

Times were tough. With my husband out of a job and our car in need of a new transmission, I could barely scrape together the money for our own Christmas dinner, let alone donate to our church's annual food drive. Their goal seemed daunting. Our Outreach Program pledged to provide forty complete food baskets to needy families in our area. "I don't think I can give much this year," I said to one of my church friends.

"Then join the packaging committee," she suggested. "They always need help coordinating and wrapping up the baskets."

That was one way to help, I thought. Yet, I wanted to do more. In past years, I had always been able to donate a full bag of groceries. So, armed with my own shopping list and the church's list of suggested donations, I drove to the supermarket one evening determined to make purchases from both. Even though I pared my own list down to the bare necessities, I came up with just enough money for one item to donate: a solitary can of cranberry sauce.

The next Sunday after services, I met with the other ladies of the packaging committee in our church basement. Sheepishly, I pushed aside the paper bag that held my single donation and went to work filling the baskets. Turkey, stuffing, juice, vegetables, condiments, and dessert were provided thanks to the generosity of our church members. As I thought of all the families that would be blessed by these baskets, I wished I could have made more of a difference.

After a busy afternoon, the last basket was about to be completed. We all stood and watched as the head of our Outreach Program prepared to tie the final ribbon. "Wait," she said, "something is missing in this basket. There's no cranberry sauce." I reached into my paper bag and produced the can. The final basket was complete.

Big or small—never underestimate the importance of your gift.

—Monica A. Andermann

December 18
The Christmas Stranger

Every year, a week before Christmas, our family presents a reenactment of the Nativity in our barn. It's a completely unrehearsed, disastrous extravaganza and features a dazzling display of costumes that include two generations of threadbare bathrobes and nightgowns and Grandma's discarded brocade draperies. The star-studded cast includes a multitude of first, second, and third cousins aged two months to eighty-five years. I suspect God winces occasionally every time He has to sit through it.

A week before the play, two carloads of aunts, uncles, cousins, and grandchildren arrive. One group descends on the barn to transform part of the haystack into steps for seating. A big stack is left in the middle so the angels can be on high, and an exquisite gold, glue-encrusted cardboard star is suspended over the manger. The other group hauls benches, tables, and chairs into the house from the storeroom.

It takes six people to bring out the old counter from our kitchen wall. It came from our great-grandfather's general store, and we can seat thirty people around it. The counter and tables are adorned with red-checked tablecloths and Christmas decorations. Fresh pine boughs are added on the day of the play. We spread sawdust on one wing of the barn floor, and the costumes are hung on a rope strung along the barn wall. One year, the sheep got in and pulled down all the costumes, so now we remember to shut the barn doors.

At dusk, the families start arriving and the barn wing becomes a three-ring circus filled with kids putting on their costumes, barking dogs, and bleating sheep. Some of the kids change costumes two or three times before they make up their minds. There are usually about twenty kids and at least that many helpers. Although there can only be one Mary, one Joseph, and one Angel Gabriel, we can have any number of shepherds, angels, Wise Men, and drummer boys. There's a part for everyone and everyone gets a part. It's a rambunctious and riotous picture of total chaos! One cousin told me she enjoyed the costume free-for-all almost as much as the play.

Popcorn and spiced cider are served to the waiting crowd who are packed on the bales of hay waiting breathlessly and wearing their warmest winter woolies. When everyone is finally ready, a hush descends on the barn, and the Angel Gabriel appears to announce the impending birth of our Savior.

We have most of the biblical animals, except for the donkey and the camel. For many years, our tiny Mary was carried to Bethlehem by our old pony, Mac. He finally succumbed at age thirty-five and had to be replaced by a life-sized homemade donkey. Our wooden, stuffed substitute will have to do until we can find a living one that can tolerate being climbed on, crawled under, patted, pinched, and poked by a swarm of children.

The camel is portrayed by two large teenagers in a home-made camel suit. The front-end teen even came home from her first year of college a day early this year so she wouldn't miss the play. The back end of the camel can always be counted on to perform a lively rendition of the Hula or the Charleston and has even been known to click its heels in the air.

The sheep, lambs, goats, and sometimes a calf are led by small shepherds. These cast members are usually coop-erative, although one year the sheep ran away and dragged the shepherds around the haystack twice before we got them under control. As we helped one little shepherd up, brushed him off, and rearranged his costume, he gasped proudly, "I didn't let go! I hung on!" He had done just that, and he had the skinned nose to prove it.

The youngest family baby is recruited to be the infant Jesus. Sometimes the "baby" climbs out of the manger before the arrival of the Wise Men (or the "wise guys," as one of our five-year-olds called them). As our eighty-five-year-old musician plays the music, an older cousin reads the Christmas story from the Bible. We all sing carols as the story unfolds, accompanied by a cow out in the corral bellowing for her missing calf. Meanwhile, on top of the haystack, the little angels are flapping their wings, turning somersaults, or picking stickers out of their underwear.

Most of the time, the play comes off without too many hitches, but if there is a problem, it usually involves the chickens. One year, the rooster hopped up on Pastor Tim's lap, and he was heard to mutter in a very unpreacher-like manner, "If you poop on my black pants, bird, you've had it!" Another time, in the middle of "Joy to the World," the rooster surrendered to a moment of uncontrollable passion with a cute little hen. By the time I pried the two birds apart, the whole place was in stitches.

During this year's production, our Angel Gabriel, wearing his silver lamé costume, stood on top of the haystack behind the little angels and did the V for Victory sign with one hand while pretending to pump iron with his other fist. Also, his wings appeared to be molting. We found white feathers all over the haystack, and our hens are all Rhode Island Reds. I think this particular angel may be demoted to passing out popcorn next Christmas.

After every play, sixty to seventy people track mud, manure, and alfalfa into the house where Pastor Tim offers up a prayer of thanksgiving for the many blessings God has bestowed on this family. Then we all sit down to a huge spaghetti dinner and await the arrival of Santa Claus. Occasionally, some child will tell Santa, "My dad has the same kind of shoes you're wearing." Another year, a child ran into the kitchen yelling, "There's a Santa Claus suit hanging in the bedroom!" Now we make sure to hide the suit in the closet.

One year, a few days before the play, my husband, Bill, came home and told me he had met an old stranger walking on the ranch and invited him to the play. The man asked Bill—in a thick accent—if he could pay him to let him walk on the ranch because the hills reminded him of his old home. Bill told the man that he didn't have to pay anything, and then he asked him where he was from.

"Russia," the stranger replied. "I was a university professor." He went on explain that he was a Christian and had been forced to worship secretly. "Things were so bad," he said, "that to keep my sanity, I would walk in the hills near my home and pray. I always feel closer to God when I am in the hills." About twenty years ago the stranger and his family were allowed to leave Russia with only ninety dollars and little else. His grown son was not allowed to leave.

Once in America, he had started at the bottom, but since he spoke three languages, he was hired by a large company as an interpreter and salesman. He prospered, and recently, he had retired in the area. "You are a Christian," the stranger said. "I can tell."

"Yes, I am," Bill replied, and the two ended up continuing their conversation over lunch.

The stranger and his wife came to the play, and Bill sat next to them on the bales of hay. When the baby Jesus was placed in the manger surrounded by the small shepherds and their animals, we all sang "Silent Night." Later, Bill told me that the stranger had sung softly in Russian as tears ran down his cheeks.

After the play, he and his wife told us how much it meant to them, and that they would never be able to do anything like this in Russia. What to us is a motley array of kids, costumes, and quirky animals is a thing of wonder to someone who has been kept from worshiping our Lord Jesus Christ.

We felt immensely blessed that God had sent the two strangers. For most of their lives, they had been deprived of the freedom to worship our Lord Jesus Christ, something we often take for granted. We also thanked God for reminding us that we live in a place that welcomes strangers when they have nothing.

—*Gigi Adam*

Salami, Cheese, and Midnight Mass

So if you sinful people know how to give good gifts to your children, how much more will your heavenly Father give good gifts to those who ask Him.
Matthew 7:11

"Mother, may I have some more salami, please? Please pass the cheese." These phrases are common, everyday phrases, but at our house, they meant Christmas Eve.

Each year, several days before Christmas, Mother would prepare homemade salami. Though the fragrance of the meat and spices would tease us for the next few days, we were not allowed to indulge until after midnight services on Christmas Eve. Oh, what a challenge that was! You see, Mother made the best homemade salami, and to wait several days was true agony.

Making the salami was my mother's gift of her talent and efforts to our family. With motherly wisdom, she knew the waiting and magical setting of our post–midnight mass family room would make it even more special.

Upon returning from midnight worship, my sisters and I would scurry into our pajamas and rush to help Mother carry the tray of cheese, crackers, and salami. With only the light from the Christmas tree, our family shared this simple feast.

All too soon, the ritual would end, and Mother and Daddy would hurry us off to bed. Santa couldn't come until we were asleep. How would we feel if children in Hawaii received their presents late because Santa was stuck waiting for us to go to bed?

I tried making salami several years ago. Though I used Mother's recipe, it didn't taste the same. Maybe my spices were old, maybe I measured incorrectly. I'm not sure what failed, but something seemed to be missing. Maybe I was simply missing Mother.

I have a child of my own now, and I think I'll try Mother's recipe this year. I'll buy fresh spices. I'll measure carefully. My family will share the snack after Christmas Eve services by the sparkling light of our own Christmas tree. No matter how the salami turns out, I bet my daughter will think it's the best ever. I wonder if the secret ingredient is simply the love between parent and child.

Though the love a mother has for her child is immeasurable, how much more must the Father love His children!

—*Susan Kneib Schank*

December 19
And a Little Child Shall Lead Them

My husband, Glen, brushed aside my appeal for help with the Christmas decorating. "I have nothing to celebrate, and besides, trees don't actually have anything to do with Christmas."

"Oh Glen, please don't be so negative," I replied. "We have a lot to celebrate. When are you going to stop playing the Grinch and help me put up this tree?"

His answer was simple and matter-of-fact. "I didn't plan on putting one up." I continued to plead. "But it's Christmas. We need to have a tree. We have to celebrate the Lord's birthday."

I decided to try a bit of reasoning. "I know it's not the tree; trees don't have a thing to do with Jesus' birthday. It's the celebration in our hearts that counts. We should let our lights shine for His glory."

Finally, my mood turned serious. "Honey, I know it's hard for you," I said. "Your daddy died last Christmas, and that would be hard on anybody." I sighed and paused for a moment. "Maybe you could look at it another way. The Lord loved your dad so much that He chose His birthday to take him home."

The expression on Glen's face told me I wasn't getting anywhere, but I couldn't stop trying to persuade him. "I loved your dad, too, but we have to go on. Christmas will be here in a week, and we haven't put up a tree, hung lights, or even bought gifts."

Almost a year had passed since my father-in-law's death, and Glen still couldn't seem to work through his grief. As the holidays grew closer, he grew more irritable. Too angry to accept the sudden death of his father the previous Christmas, his rage continued to build within him. "I might have to go on, but I don't have to celebrate the day I lost my father," he said and stalked out the door.

My heart ached for him. I needed to find a way to bring Christmas back into my home. Glen couldn't live with this bitterness and, frankly, neither could I. After giving my dilemma a great deal of thought, an idea came to me. We needed a child to put life back into our home. God chose His child to put salvation into the hearts of man. A child is what we needed for the holidays.

It hadn't been part of God's plan for us to have a child of our own, so I prayed He would allow us to find one who might need us for Christmas. With only a week left, I scrutinized the yellow pages in search of a program that might give me an inkling of where to begin. I found nothing and turned to the government pages without success.

I contacted Child Welfare to find out if we might get a foster child for a couple of days. I learned that being approved for foster care was a long, drawn-out process, and it would entail a longer commitment than just the Christmas holidays. We had discussed adopting a baby someday, not fostering an adolescent.

I wasn't about to give up, so I began calling everyone possible in the city offices. Finally, someone in the mayor's office told me about the Kentucky Children's Home. The Home needed couples to sponsor children for Christmas and possibly other holidays. It would only be for a few days, and then the child would return to the Home, while we returned to our normal lives.

I was certain this would be a great way to get past the holiday that had left a void in my husband's heart. I didn't tell Glen about my plans until the last minute, but surprisingly, he didn't object. "That might be fun," he said. "I guess we could put up a tree just for a few days. That's all it is, right? I don't want to commit to a long-term arrangement."

I nodded. "Just for the holidays."

On December 23, 1970, we drove to the Kentucky Children's Home. Billy was a skinny, bright-eyed, ten-year-old filled with energy and questions. We were allowed to take him out for dinner, and he chose Pizza Hut. With a mouth full of pepperoni and cheese, he gazed first at me and then at Glen. "Do you think you might adopt me?" he said.

Glen took a quick drink of water, while I swallowed an unchewed piece of sausage. "You might want to be careful with that question," I replied. "You could end up with a family you don't want." I side-stepped my reply to his question, since he looked like the type of child that wouldn't take "no" for an answer.

There was time for a little window shopping before we took him back to the Home. We needed to know what sort of thing appealed to a ten-year-old. After promising to pick him up on Christmas Eve, we drove back to the mall and loaded up with toys. It was wonderful to see Glen as excited as I was.

There was no room in our house for negativity that Christmas. Our home and hearts were full of joy as we watched Billy's eyes illuminate and sparkle like the lights on the tree when he tore away the paper and opened one present after another.

It seemed only natural that we should invite Billy over to play with the toys he hadn't been allowed to take back to the Children's home. There were strict rules on how many presents the sponsored children could have at the orphanage. Those children who weren't lucky enough to leave for the holidays only received twenty dollars worth of toys. It wouldn't be fair for the children chosen to leave the premises to have an abundance of toys, while the others had only a few.

Then, it was only natural that we should bring him home with us every holiday such as Easter, Thanksgiving, the Fourth of July, and his birthday. Before long, we kept him every day he wasn't in school, even over the summer break.

About six months later, it seemed reasonable for Billy to move in with us as a foster child. The application was rather simple since we were his sponsors already. After two Christmases had passed, it felt completely right when he became Glen Kinsey, Jr., our adopted son. We just knew he wasn't the type of child to accept "no" for an answer.

—Jean Kinsey

The Lord's Cup

Should we accept only good things from the hand of God and never anything bad?
JOB 2:10

When the Christmas holidays approach, many people serve different brews. There are many new designer teas, hot cinnamon apple cider, and more coffees around than Juan Valdez ever dreamed of when Starbucks opened. My personal favorite is a hot steaming cup of Colombian coffee.

With the theme of cups, I think of my growing collection of them. My best friend brought me one from Greece, and I have a beautiful gold-trimmed teacup my sister-in-law gave me from her own collection. Then, there is a cup from Cracker Barrel that my husband bought me and my assorted collection of china cups. One favorite is a mug that my mother gave me when I had my second child twenty-one years after my first. It read, "I'm a new Mom!" At age thirty-six, I felt pretty old to be new, but now that Mama is gone, I treasure it.

What is in the cup the Lord has given you this year? Has the drink been as warm and sweet as the coffee that is handed to children, filled with milk and sugar and only a hint of the brew inside? Was your year as fragrant as peppermint tea? Was it as spicy as the hot chili my Mama used to make? Was it as bitter as a hot medicine you forced yourself to choke down in order to soothe a sore throat?

I still remember the year we had one of the best Christmas celebrations ever. It was nearly picture perfect, and I thank the Lord for that gift.

However, lives are not always picture perfect, and the reality of life is that only Jesus satisfies. The cup He has allowed in my life this year is bittersweet, but I still believe He can bring our lives full circle to His will.

Accept the Lord's cup as part of His perfect plan for your life.

—*Donna Collins Tinsely*

December 20
The Christmas Story Tree

My grandmother pulled a nativity ornament out of a box. "Who is this?" she asked.

"Baby Jesus." I answered, delighted as any four-year-old who knew the right answer.

"Now say a Bible verse that goes along with it."

"They hurried to the village and found Mary and Joseph," I replied. "And there was the baby, lying in the manger. Luke 2:16"

My grandmother placed the resin ornament in my hands. "Good, now you can hang it on the tree."

I believed that if I fell or dropped it, I might hurt the Baby Jesus, so I walked carefully to the tree and hung it on the best limb a child could find.

Our Christmas Story Tree was a tradition passed down from long ago. My grandmother taught me the Christmas story through the special tree ornaments that had been made or inherited from past generations. Making new ornaments was a family project done on a Saturday after the Thanksgiving holiday. When we went out to shop for Christmas, she would remind us to keep our eyes open for any religious ornaments available. When I was small, those items were rare, and if we did find a display, many times they weren't available for purchase.

Pine cone photo frames, craft sticks, and paper snowflakes adorned the tree as I graduated from elementary school to middle school. My mother dated each one and kept them protected from the elements when they were packed away after the season.

Not only did my family hang my school ornaments, but also those collected to represent the special times of our lives. For example, my grandfather bought an ornament while on a trip in Florida. He said he purchased it because he thought the seashell was cute, but we knew the real reason. He never wanted to forget how lonely or homesick he was without my grandmother. For the rest of their lives together, he never took another trip without her by his side.

When I became a teenager and my grandmother's health began to fail, it was my mother's turn to pull each fragile ornament from its box. As each one emerged, I recited a Bible verse and placed it on the tree. My mother joined my grandmother on the couch to oversee the tradition. When I forgot the proper wording of a verse, my grandmother would either call my grandfather, a pastor for more than forty years, or open the Bible and ask me to look it up and read it aloud.

By the time I reached eighteen, religious ornaments were becoming more popular, and my family purchased nativities, angels, crosses, and other symbols of the Christian faith. Each year, as our tree became more decorated, my knowledge of the scripture pertaining to the Christmas Story grew.

At twenty-three, I became a mother and I realized the significance of our Christmas Story Tree. I wanted my oldest son, Robert, to understand the real reason we celebrate Christmas. As soon as he could understand, I introduced him to our Christmas Story Tree and began asking him the same questions my grandmother had asked me. "Who is this? What is a Bible verse that would go along with this ornament?"

When Robert was six years old, his father and I divorced. That Christmas, I decided we would skip the Christmas Story Tree for a more modern and elegant one. We needed to make new memories. In September, I began my search for the perfect ornaments. I found a beautiful blue Christmas topper, ball ornaments, and bows that matched. I splurged on hand-spun glass hearts and crosses, as well as brass musical instruments for the tree. To tie all the colors together, I purchased hand-woven tinsel and a matching tree skirt. For me, the tree was absolutely gorgeous.

After Thanksgiving dinner, we all gathered to decorate the tree. When I began opening the boxes containing the new ornaments, silence filled the room. However, in a matter of moments, the questions began to fly thick and fast.

"What are you doing?"

"I understand about making new memories, but why change our tree?"

"What does a blue ornament have to do with the Christmas Story?"

At some point during my explanation of the need for change, Robert found the box full of our Christmas Story ornaments and brought it into the room. "Here Mom," he said as he pulled the Baby Jesus in the manger out of its container. "I don't know the verse."

My heart sank. "Honey, we're changing the tree this year. We're going to have a more up-to-date tree, okay?" My mother looked at me, cocked her eyebrow, shook her head, and left the room.

Rob drew his eyebrows together in confusion. "Why?" he asked.

"I just want to try something different."

"Mom, we don't need a new tree. I like the old one." His bottom lip began to tremble.

I was determined to have my elegant tree. "Robert, we're having new decorations this year."

"I want my Granny's tree!"

"Not this year, young man."

He put the ornament back in its box and ran from the room. A few minutes later, I heard him playing cars. My mother had joined both of my grandparents in the den to watch television. Looking around the room, I realized no one stayed to help with the new decorations. I finished the tree alone. I couldn't understand why no one wanted to change.

A few days after I decorated the tree, I began to notice the appearance of our family ornaments. Some were hung on branches in the back, and others placed deep inside the tree where they couldn't be seen without close inspection.

I found Robert's favorite ornament, Baby Jesus in a manger, hidden behind a branch. I removed it and told him to come in the room.

When he entered and saw the ornament in my hand, his steps slowed. "Mom, I like the Baby Jesus."

"I do too, son."

He took it out of my hand and said, "They hurried to the village and found Mary and Joseph. And there was the baby, lying in the manger. Luke 2:16."

"Very good. Now, you may hang it on the tree."

He started to place it in the back of the tree where he had hidden it.

"No, wait," I said. "I can't see it back there." He laughed and hung it in the front. Then, he left the room and returned with the box full of the Christmas Story Tree ornaments.

"Go and get your grandmother, young man. We have a lot of ornaments to hang."

"Granny," he shouted, and I heard her hurry down the hallway. Robert ran to meet her. "We're going to decorate the tree."

I looked up as he pulled her into the room. Once she realized what was happening, she picked up the Bible and sat in her place on the couch.

That afternoon, Robert's innocence was my wake-up call. I realized there were more important memories associated with our Christmas Story Tree than any new ones I wanted to make.

Since that time, I remarried and had another son, Jared. When he became old enough we began to teach him the Bible verses that my family associated with each ornament. Now, both my sons are grown and Robert is engaged to be married. Someday, I'll be sitting on the couch and watching my grandchildren gently remove each ornament from their respective boxes, reciting verses, and hanging them on the tree just as my children did.

My grandmother passed away when Robert was eight. I know she is in heaven overseeing our ceremony as she did in years past. She would be glad to know that the Christmas Story is being taught the same way she taught me—with faith, love, and family tradition.

—Katie Lovette

The Rock People

Because of God's tender mercy,
the morning light from heaven is about to break upon us,
to give light to those who sit in darkness and in the
shadow of death,
and to guide us to the path of peace.
LUKE 1:78–79

It happened again this year at our family's Christmas celebration. Someone said, "Remember the year when Ann made our presents?" We laughed and reminisced of a Christmas twenty-seven years ago.

That December, five-year-old Ann sulked. "I don't have any presents to give," she said. For several weeks, her older brothers and sisters, who had jobs and salaries, had been coming home with bags of mysterious contents. "Don't you dare peek," they admonished as they stashed the packages in closets. Ann felt left out of the holiday excitement.

In an effort to console her, I said, "You could make gifts."

I didn't think Ann would take on the task, but I was wrong. She flew to her room and came back with markers, a skein of yarn, and a bottle of Elmer's glue. Then she disappeared outside on the Arizona desert landscape. In half an hour she was back and announced, "I've got Christmas presents made for everyone. They're a secret. I'm not showing anyone until Christmas."

On Christmas Eve, Ann's three brothers, two sisters, her dad, and I opened packages that revealed rock people complete with marker faces and yellow yarn hair.

In the years that followed, family members received many gifts from Ann, all more costly than rocks. Yet, every Christmas when we gathered, we talked about the wonderful rock people she gave us that year.

Her simple gifts invariably remind us of another gift, the one from God. No one paid much attention to Mary and Joseph searching through Bethlehem's crowded streets looking for a room. Only shepherds took note of the baby lying in a stable. Centuries later, people don't talk much about King Herod or Caesar Augustus's census decree, or Quirinius, the governor of Syria. Still, from countless pulpits we hear messages of the gift God gave us in such a simple way. Reverberating through malls and on city streets are songs of the infant Messiah God sent to the world.

Keep Christmas simple and quiet, without frills—like Ann's gifts. Perhaps that's the way God intended the birthday of His Son to be celebrated.

A simple gift can speak volumes about love.

—*Jewell Johnson*

December 21
The Night the Sheep Got Sheared

"Angels and lambs, ladybugs and fireflies . . ." The sanctuary filled with the pure, sweet sound of children's voices. My first- and second-grade choir joined the rest of the school that afternoon, singing and gesturing their hearts out at the final dress rehearsal for our upcoming Christmas pageant. It was an amazing sight, but the most amazing thing of all was squeezing 103 adorned and adorable creatures from the four- to eleven-year-old combined choirs onto one rather small stage.

My young choir had been assigned to play lambs and fireflies. The children could decide which animal they wanted to be, and their parents could choose how to create their costumes. As you might imagine, there was everything from simple to elaborate—all with one thing in common: they topped the charts in cuteness.

That afternoon, as I took my place up front among the other directors, ready to lead our groups through the dress rehearsal, my eyes fell on two little sisters from my choir. Jennie and Janie's costumes weren't finished. My heart had gone out to them from the moment I discovered that their mother had run away from home in April. I knew the girls' father was doing his best to be both mommy and daddy to his daughters. I recalled a phone conversation with him two weeks earlier.

"Roger," I said, "did you get my recent letter to parents about the costumes?"

"Yep, we need two lamb costumes, right?"

I gulped, knowing he was the engineer of the family, and his wife had been the creative one. "Yes, in fact I'm calling to tell you I'd consider it a privilege if you'd let me make the girls' costumes."

His response was swift and determined. "Actually, I'm making them myself. Got it all planned. Thanks anyway!" He assured me he had already started the project, and then he politely dismissed my offer. Who was I to stand in the way of designer wooly-wear, dutifully engineered by a brilliant mind and a loving heart?

Pageant night bleated and buzzed its way into our busy Christmas schedules almost without warning, and there we were, wall-to-wall lambs and fireflies, squeals of excitement, and a decibel level our choir room had never known. But where were Jennie and Janie? It was almost time to line up to go into the auditorium. I pictured a panicky dad, tearful girls, and a last minute costume crisis. What to do? I couldn't go in without them. I wouldn't.

Just then, they burst into the room, huffing and puffing, faces beaming, and clutching two large bags. I watched as their daddy bent down to hug them. He stroked their hair and smiled into their eyes.

"Bye now," he whispered. "Daddy will be watching. I'm so proud of you." He straightened up, gave me a huge grin and a "thumbs up" sign—as if he had just completed his one hundredth combat mission. Then, he scooted out toward the auditorium.

Combat mission indeed! When the girls opened their bags to reveal their lamb costumes, it looked like an explosion had occurred at the cotton ball factory. As I gingerly lifted out the two masterpieces, I marveled at what must have been hundreds, maybe thousands of cotton balls super-glued to two large white plastic garbage bags with holes cut out for their heads and arms.

"My daddy made this all by himself!" Jennie said.

"Look!" Janie added, "I'm really wooly!"

My assistant and I carefully dressed these two precious little lambs, put them at the head of the line, and led all our bouncy, bedecked creatures single-file into the auditorium. I followed behind the last little firefly, his miniature flashlight illuminating the path for me.

As it turned out, light wasn't the only thing that covered the path. With each step of our trek from the choir room to the auditorium, a bizarre version of Hansel and Gretel began to play out as I spotted one cotton ball, then another, and another. More and more cotton balls appeared along the "trail," leading me to a sight I wouldn't soon forget.

That was the night I discovered a new definition of a millisecond—the amount of time it takes for a bazillion cotton balls to liberate themselves from the grip of superglue. Without fanfare, they completed their freedom flight from white bag to crimson carpet . . . two by two, four by four . . . ten by ten . . . little Kamikaze cotton balls everywhere but where they were supposed to be. By the time Jennie and Janie climbed onto the stage, they were wearing plain, white garbage bags without a cotton ball in sight.

I saw their two faces beaming, and my heart sank. Surely, they didn't know yet that their wool had been sheared. I couldn't bear to look at their daddy, who had painstakingly, singlehandedly, glued each white round ball onto the now-bare bags. I could only imagine how he felt when he saw them. All his futile efforts and wasted hours, carved out of an already overloaded schedule.

When I finally mustered up the courage to find him in the crowd, I was unprepared for what I saw. He was sporting a wide smile and twinkling eyes. He wasn't looking at the costumes. He was gazing into the eyes of his precious little lambs, whose dimpled grins stood out to him from among the 103 assorted creatures. With sweet, lilting voices, cherub faces, and lively gestures all the animals sang,

Angels and lambs, lady bugs and fireflies told everybody in sight
That Jesus was born in Bethlehem, on that starry night!

It was an amazing evening on many levels: the mouths of babes proclaiming God's message of love, His creatures, fluttering, flying, leaping, and crawling around the manger, excited about the birth of Jesus, and in the midst of it all, God showing me yet another picture of true love.

I had been so worried what the girls might do when they realized what had happened to their costumes, but my concern was unnecessary. In pure childlike fashion, their giggles followed the trail of snowy-white cotton back to the choir room after the program. Then it dawned on me, as clearly as the collective light from our super-sized fireflies. The costumes were unimportant. What really mattered was what their daddy had done. Every minute, every cotton ball, every drop of glue provided proof of his love for his girls. They must have felt so cherished.

And what about their dad? If he did notice the bare bags adorning his daughters onstage, he didn't seem to care. All that captured his attention were their angelic smiles. He was one proud papa.

As I swept up the last of the cotton balls that night, I was tempted to wrap them up and save them, so I could pull them out whenever I questioned God's love for His children. In one heavenly night that Christmas season, He gave me two priceless gifts: a new set of eyes, and a fresh understanding about where to focus them.

How many times had the eyes of my heart failed to see what was really important? Did I get so caught up in trying to perform and earn God's gifts, that I missed the unconditional love behind each one? How often had I agonized over the reactions of others and their assumptions about what I did or didn't do for my children? As a young mother, how many times had I fixed my gaze on the projects that backfired, my flaws and my failings, and in doing so, completely missed the beauty and wonder of my child?

I may be a silly sentimentalist, but I turn into one giant goose bump every time I think back on that colorful assortment of squealy, squirmy creatures. Not only did they proclaim God's message of hope through the wondrous birth of the Christ child, but also they managed to wriggle their way into my heart and make an impact on my life that has spanned the decades—especially two little girls who proudly wore their father's labor of love.

—*Sandi L. Banks*

The First G.P.S. (Global Positioning Star)

*The star which they saw in the east, went before them, till it
came and stood over where the young child was.*
MATTHEW 3:9

We took the train from Washington to California to spend
Christmas with my mom and dad. My husband, Keith, had
just bought a new "toy"—a Global Positioning System
guaranteed to tell you where you are, where you want to
be, and the distance from your destination.

The train meandered through the snow-covered mountains, and to break the monotony, Keith would tell me where
we were and the location of the nearest town. The G.P.S.
worked well most of the time, until we got out of range of
the satellite or found ourselves in a tunnel.

Childhood memories of Christmas past whirled
through my mind as we traveled to our Christmas reunion.
I thought about the G.P.S. (Global Positioning Star). It
was the biggest and most spectacular star ever to appear in
the heavens. The Wise Men knew the prophecies, and if
something strange or different appeared in the skies, they
noticed. When they looked up and saw the star, they were
as excited as any astronomer would be by the discovery of
something new in the heavens.

The Wise Men were well aware of this star's significance. It was so important that they hopped on their trusty camels and traveled for days to follow the star. They didn't take off in some haphazard fashion; they had a plan. They brought marvelous gifts to pay tribute to the miracle waiting for them beneath the star.

Our man-made G.P.S. isn't flawless. It depends on a signal and perfect circumstances, but the G.P.S. that the Wise Men followed was constant and trustworthy. It never wavered, and it didn't have to be recharged or rely on batteries. It was powered by the everlasting power source of the creator.

God is the ultimate G.P.S.

—*Midge DeSart*

December 22
The Magi Who Purred

The smell of a warm and toasty cat wafted through the house. We knew it came from Eddie, my tiger-striped alley cat who loved to sleep in the nativity scene, under the blue Christmas bulb that simulated starlight shining on the Baby Jesus. I looked at my mother. Her lips puckered as she frowned, but I thought I saw a sparkle in her hazel eyes. At seventeen, I had learned that not every stern look was for real. I smiled at her mock scowl, and then, we both laughed about Eddie's choice of beds. It hadn't always been so comical.

Mom first brought the ceramic nativity set home when I was in my early teens, and we put it up on the floor, under the Christmas tree, exclaiming over the intricate detail on the pieces. I loved the serene faces of the Wise Men and imagined the love in their hearts as they extended their gifts to the Baby Jesus. Stroking the donkey and sheep, I put them in what I thought must be just the right places, where a donkey and sheep should stand to give homage and to exalt the Lord our God!

It didn't take long before we'd arranged all the statues, plugged in the bulb, and started the music box at the rear of the stable. As we stepped back to admire our work, the sweet, tinkling sound of "Silent Night" floated from the nativity and filled the room.

Because of the music, we didn't hear Eddie pussyfooting in behind us. With a stealth that's second nature to cats, he waited until we turned our backs and then slunk into the stable, nudging pieces aside until he'd settled himself next to the Baby Jesus.

The music box gave its final ping, and I turned around to rewind it. Eddie stared at me and flipped the tip of his dark tail several times. I knew from experience that particular gesture was cat body language for, "It will require a long pry bar and three brave men to remove me from my place."

"Bad cat!" I said, as I reached over and tried to shoo him away. He wedged his chubby body in tighter and curled his sharp claws in preparation for a struggle. I snapped my fingers softly several times and then drummed them along the blue-green carpet, hoping to entice him into chasing my hand. "Come on, Eddie. Come out of there."

He gazed at me as if I were transparent, and then gave me a long, slow blink that seemed to say, "I'm ignoring you."

My folks both worked full-time because money was tight in the sixties. I knew, from the feel of the painted statues and the thickness of the wooden stable, that the nativity scene wasn't one of those cheap dime-store models. I could only imagine what the set had cost, and I didn't want pieces broken, or the wooden stable smashed to bits by the exuberance of a hefty cat.

Despite my love for Eddie, I reached in, gently took him by the scruff of the neck, and worked his resistive torso back out. Setting him on the oak hardwood floor, I gave him a pat on the head and a small push from behind, hoping he would meander into my lilac-colored bedroom and entertain himself with his favorite pastime—knocking everything off my dresser and onto the floor.

He shot me an indignant stare in return for what was obviously perceived as treatment unworthy of feline royalty. After all, his full name was Oedipus Rex, a moniker given to him by me. I'd found him in the backyard of our small home in the Washington, D.C. suburbs and wheedled my folks into letting me keep him. Had I known the story of Oedipus the King marring his mother and killing his father, I never would have named him that. Still, as a young teenager, the name sounded regal to me, and it certainly suited a cat who woke everyone up at four in the morning and then curled up, nose to tail, and went back to sleep.

Eddie sashayed away, his tail flicking back and forth with insolence. "Go play," I said as a parting retort. "And don't climb back into that nativity set again!" With that, I considered settled the issue of "the cat that didn't belong in the crèche."

An hour later, I walked in to find him asleep in the dark wooden stable under the Christmas tree, his face close to the smiling, haloed baby, and his steady purr emitting a soft rumble.

The scene repeated itself throughout most of the holiday season. I'd cajole, push, or pull him from among the statues, only to find him there later, his gold eyes gleaming by the light of the blue bulb. Eventually, he won the battle. Mom and I gave up because we actually found his persistence and stubbornness funny. He inhabited the nativity scene daily until we took the decorations down after Mom's birthday, on January 6.

That first year, we thought the bulb was the key. All cats love warmth, and we decided he crept into the crèche for the heat. However, as the years went by, we realized that even when the bulb wasn't turned on, he still curled up in the stable. Sometimes, he would knock over a statue, but most of the time, he picked his way carefully between them, wrapped his body this way and that around the wise men, shepherds and livestock, and then snuggled in, his front paws touching the baby in the manger.

Many times, I'd wind up the music box and the chiming melody of "Silent Night" would mingle with Eddie's purrs. It became the sound of Christmas to me.

I'm a grandmother now, and Eddie is no longer with us. During the bustle of the days before Christmas, when I see live nativities, I often smile and think of how we had the first live nativity—minus braying donkeys and baaing sheep—with a pudgy, purring cat. Sometimes, I wonder if he knew more than we gave him credit for, if perhaps he held an innate understanding of what too many people today have forgotten.

The nativity set now resides with my son and his family. They put it out yearly, and when I walk past it, I envision Eddie, intertwined among the statues, rumbling his love to Jesus in the manger. The traditional story tells about three Wise Men visiting the Messiah, but in my life there were four—Gaspar, Melcior, Balthasar, and Eddie. They came bearing gifts of gold, frankincense, myrrh . . . and purr.

—*Cindy Beck*

A Family Celebration

Once you had no identity as a people;
now you are God's people.
Once you received no mercy;
now you have received God's mercy.
1 PETER 2:10

There's nothing worse than to arrive at the end of Christmas Eve and realize that everything you've done that day has little to do with the birth of Jesus. Yet, that's exactly what happened to me.

I started out with great plans. Our family would sing Christmas carols around the piano, and our oldest son would read the Christmas story found in the book of Luke. We would turn out the lights and use candles as we each gave thanks to God for the marvelous gift of His Son. Then, we would open presents and delight in our love for one another.

We never got to the Christmas story, and we never sang carols around the piano. I found myself stuck in the kitchen, either serving up food or washing dishes in order to serve up more food. Plenty of laughter erupted from the other room, but I never once heard a prayer. We opened gifts before it got too late for the little ones to enjoy it. By the time I saw everyone out the door and my husband Cat had crawled into bed, my heart ached with a profound emptiness.

"I'm heading out," I told Cat. Then, I drove to the midnight service at the Catholic Church. I felt awkward and alone. I usually attend a nondenominational church, but our service had ended hours ago.

As I walked up the steps, I whispered a prayer, "Please help me to sit next to someone who loves you as much as I do." I was shocked by the size of the crowd filling the church as the usher seated me. I had no idea so many people attended church at midnight. An old man with shaking hands shared his hymnal with me, and in the vastness of that tall cathedral, he and I poured our hearts out to the Lord. Praises rang throughout the rafters, and it was easy to imagine the angels singing on that first Christmas night.

Christmas celebrates the wonder of family—not just our blood families, but also the worldwide family that the birth of God's Son made possible.

It is a joy to celebrate Christmas with the family of God.

—*Sandy Cathcart*

December 23
Christmas Spirit—
Lost and Found

*M*y dream of the perfect Christmas Eve consists of attending the seven o'clock evening service at my church (not too early or too late), singing lots of my favorite carols, and feeling warm and fuzzy from the pastor's concise, yet meaningful, message. My fantasy ends with candlelight and singing "Silent Night," and as the carol softly echoes in my spirit, I drift home full of peace.

Being in charge of the worship pageant this year past blew any possibility that this Christmas would live up to my ideal scenario.

"I don't believe it!" I said.

"What's wrong?" my husband, Phil, asked.

"Why can't I have a nice, quiet Christmas Eve? After all the decorating at the church, now I've been asked to do something more. I'm tired of all the preparation."

"What now?"

"I've told you how I have to tell the shepherds, angels, and everyone else what to do at the Christmas Eve services."

Phil's sigh seemed a lot deeper than it needed to be. "Yes," he replied. "Many times."

"Well, I had hoped to slip into the end of the seven o'clock service and enjoy what I could of the candle lighting and singing."

"So, what's wrong?"

"I just got an e-mail from the pastor. Her husband isn't feeling well, and she asked if I could go to the parsonage Christmas Eve about seven-thirty and help set up the open house refreshments. I couldn't say no."

An understanding smile appeared on Phil's face. "Well, it was your choice."

It was my turn to sigh. "I know. Where is that quiet time to experience the Christmas spirit?"

He gave me a hug. "It will all work out. I'll help you out at the parsonage."

Christmas Eve day arrived, and my mind overflowed with worries about costumes, people showing up, and how long I would last before I collapsed.

At four, the children's choir gathered to practice in the parlor for the five o'clock children's service. With angel gowns, shepherd robes, head mantles, and halos dangling from my hands, I staggered into the parlor. I handed over the costumes to the choir and dashed back to the chapel, my command center, to check my list.

I paced as I waited for the couple and baby who would play the holy family. Four days before, the original couple had cancelled. I knew only one other young couple, and much to my relief, they were thrilled by the opportunity to participate. They arrived at the chapel, dressed quickly, and swathed their baby, Jenna, in gauze. I know what you're thinking, but no one says that a boy has to represent baby Jesus.

At five o'clock, parents and excited children filled the sanctuary. The angels and shepherds skipped and swaggered in to sing, and then they sat and sprawled on the steps below the crèche and stool where Mary would sit. The holy family entered as the congregation sang "Away in a Manger."

When the pastor invited the children to come to see the baby Jesus, something magical happened. The children rushed forward and parents with infants and toddlers held them up close to the tiny Jesus. I watched from the back, mesmerized by the glow of the church lights around the children.

The entire cast returned to the chapel, and I was busy again as I removed costumes, and calmed and herded the shepherds and angels while they waited to sing another song. Soon, everyone was singing "Silent Night," the flickering flames of their candles illuminating the darkened sanctuary.

A peaceful hush filled the sanctuary as the parents and children left. Then, I heard laughter and voices as everyone began to call out Christmas greetings to each other. Phil found me in the chapel preparing for the seven o'clock service, listening to the happy exchanges in the hall.

"That was hectic," I said. I took his hand, and we wandered into the church office. "Weren't the children wonderful gathered around baby Jesus?" I asked Phil as we munched on some cookies we discovered—our supper.

"Pastor Caroline told me she'd do it for the next service, too," he replied, "but there will be fewer young children."

At six-thirty, young people home from college and visiting grandparents started to arrive. The second service had fewer participants, so two of the acolytes were recruited as shepherds and the holy family's four-year-old was enlisted as an angel.

"Elizabeth," I pleaded, "you'd be a beautiful angel. Let's put this white tunic on and you can pretend you have wings."

With encouragement from her parents, Elizabeth put on the tunic and became a very active and verbal angel, flying around the chapel as her parents transformed her little brother into the infant Jesus.

The acolytes walked sedately to the front and lit the candles, but only one came back. "Where's my sister?" Molly asked.

"I thought she was going to come back with you," I replied, a note of desperation in my voice. I couldn't afford to lose even one of my two shepherds. We looked up and down the church aisles, but no Mandy. We finally spotted her sitting in the choir loft behind the pastor. She had remained there after lighting the candles just as she did on Sundays.

"Don't worry, Molly," I said. "I'm sure she'll join the holy family when they come down the aisle."

Time for the holy family's entrance arrived, and Mandy, the wayward shepherd, moved into position. Molly started to stroll down the aisle expecting Elizabeth to follow. Suddenly, Elizabeth noticed that her mother and father weren't with her, and the once lively angel froze.

I put my hands on her shoulders and used my most encouraging voice. "Go on, Elizabeth. "Do you see Molly? She's beckoning for you to come." I gave her a little push past the first pews and crept up behind her. "Look," I said. Your mom and dad are up front. They're waiting for you."

I gave her another little push, and finally, Elizabeth's feet started to inch forward.

There were no flapping arms or little dances, as Elizabeth slowly shuffled to the front as everyone in the congregation watched her progress and smiled. Joseph, also known as "Daddy," soon had Elizabeth in hand, and the tableau was complete.

This time, when the pastor invited the children to come see Jesus, there was silence, and then one mother carried her little boy down to the front. The child reached toward Jesus, obviously captivated by this special personal moment.

Soon the holy family was back in the chapel to return their costumes.

Phil came up behind me as I finished folding the last set of clothes. "Time to go, Princess," he said. "It's seven-thirty."

I looked longingly at the people enjoying the rest of the service for a moment before Phil and I hurried across the street to the parsonage, shivering from the icy wind and blowing snow.

Our pastor's husband, Bill, greeted us. "Come on in," he said. "Hang your coats in the closet. When we run out of room there, they can go in the bedroom upstairs."

"Show us what we need to do, then you can sit and rest before the other folks arrive," I replied. Soon, we were bustling around the pastor's kitchen as if it were our own. In twenty minutes, everything was ready for the guests.

The doorbell rang, and I ran to welcome the first of the Christmas Eve visitors. Pastor Caroline appeared, and soon the house was full of conversation and laughter. I stayed near the door to greet new arrivals, occasionally returning to the kitchen and dining room to check on refills. It's fun playing hostess, I thought. It was beginning to feel a lot more like Christmas.

After the last guest left, we helped clear empty cups and plates, said our goodbyes, and walked back to the church to get our car. The inky black sky shimmered with brilliant sparks of light, radiant and beautiful in the frigid air. Holding hands, we crunched our way through the snow to the car without speaking.

"You're awfully quiet," Phil said as he gently turned me around to face him.

"I'm drifting in the peace."

"Peace?"

"When I've dreamed of my ideal Christmas, I drift home full of peace."

"Don't tell me you've found the Christmas spirit."

I countered his teasing with a grin. "I think it found me. It beckoned to me through the countless Christmas greetings, it led me into worship through the holy families that walked down the aisles, it danced around me through candle and starlight, and finally, it caught up with me when I answered the door at the parsonage and refilled food on the table."

Phil gave me a quick kiss. "Merry Christmas, Princess."

"A very Merry Christmas, indeed."

—*Laurie A. Perkins*

A Widow's Christmas

Father to the fatherless, defender of widows—
this is God, whose dwelling is holy.
God places the lonely in families;
he sets the prisoners free and gives them joy.
PSALM 68:5–6

The traditional Christmas lamps at the church were twinkling, and the tree decorations shone against the evergreen. The music was swelling for the conclusion of my husband's funeral service on December 23. The pastor had offered to remove the Christmas decorations, but I wanted them left in place, as I saw my husband off on his new life.

My stepdaughter, Mary, was at my side. "Now, you will come home with me for Christmas." I had many offers for Christmas, but it was right to spend it with Mary's family. I needed to be with someone who had loved Dean even before I knew him.

It was a long drive, over three states, in glistening snow and ice. At Mary's house, where Dean and I had frequently visited, the family dog leaped to greet me as I stepped from the car. My young stepgrandson, Ty, was more subdued, but he knew instinctively what I needed.

After I unpacked, he was at the door of my room, "Grandmother, would you like a chess game?"

Since I was competing with a nine-year-old, I played casually and didn't attempt any tricky moves. I got whipped! I put my mind firmly on the next game, playing with all my skill. This time I won, but not easily.

The food, the conversation, the tree, helping Mary display her illuminated "Dickens Village" all made it a Christmas to remember. At dinner, the large family of Mary's husband, Jimmy, all made me feel welcome. Just the sight of the Blue Ridge Mountains from the window was enough to lift my spirits.

I was invited to share in everything, but nothing was forced. There was time for healthy grief, but no time to wallow in self-pity. When the time came for me to return to my empty house, I was fortified.

Love and families are where you find them, as God's free gift.

—*Edith Tyson Bell*

December 24
Gloria

Our community buzzed with the news. Gerald, one of our hometown boys, had met and married a girl named Gloria while he was on extended leave in England during World War II.

Long before she and their infant son came to Canada to join him after he was discharged, we sensed that Gloria was different. If people asked, and only when they did, Gerald showed them his wedding picture. They were both in their early thirties, Gerald still in uniform, his bride wearing a simple afternoon dress and pillbox hat tipped slightly to the side. She carried a small white Bible overlaid with lilies of the valley. She looked pleasant enough, and the community anticipated her arrival with typical small-town curiosity.

Intent upon seeing what *she* was like, none of us on the platform of the CNR train station, on that day in 1946, thought to look at the scene from Gloria's perspective. Our village was no more than a scattering of frame houses huddled on the north side of the railway track. It was September, and the Paterson elevator was digesting a steady diet of grain trucks. One by one, they groaned up the steep incline to its weigh scale and were swallowed by its yawning doors. Relieved of their loads and discharged out the other side, they rattled away empty down gravel roads.

A team of horses, intimidated by the whistle of the approaching train, jerked and strained at their hitching post in front of the general store. Anticipating a shipment of block salt and Macintosh apples, the storekeeper had pushed his wheelbarrow across the cinder pathway to the railway station and parked it on the loading platform beside the self-appointed welcoming committee.

Women in print housedresses and gingham aprons stood in little groups bearing gifts of cream and eggs and baked goods. Grizzled farmers, their plaid shirts stained by perspiration, peered down the train track. Impatient to get back to their harvesting, they anxiously consulted the pocket watches they carried in the bib pockets of their blue denim overalls.

As the steam locomotive hissed to a stop, pupils who had slipped away from the nearby school grounds during lunch hour stared wide eyed as the baggage men unloaded three trunks and two leather suitcases. A mangy dog that bounded up to sniff the Macintosh apples was swiftly discouraged from any further intentions by a deft kick delivered off the toe of a gum rubber boot.

And then at the far end of the platform we caught sight of the conductor. Emerging from the end coach, he positioned the little step stool and turned to assist the first passenger. As Gloria stepped down with her baby in her arms, Gerald wrapped his arms around them both in a self-conscious embrace. As he turned to introduce her, the motley little crowd surged forward to greet her, and then they hesitated. She was meticulously dressed in a red wool suit and hat, her son in white satin rompers.

Most of us had never seen such fine clothing, and at the last moment, the calloused hands and gnarled fingers that had been stretched out to offer hearty greetings were self-consciously withdrawn. Gerald tried his best to smooth over the awkwardness of the situation, but Gloria posed a problem these plain farm folk had never encountered. She was, in their words, "too classy." Her three trunks and two suitcases contained more beautiful clothes and china than most rural women ever dreamed of owning. She dressed her baby in silks and satins, crooned him to sleep with strange melodies, refused visitors if it was inconvenient and seemed offended by homemade tokens of love. People concluded that Gerald had married rich.

The autumn ebbed away into winter and undaunted by Gloria's chilly attitude, community women tried to break down the barriers one by one.

Christmas arrived, and Gerald and Gloria were invited to attend the annual Christmas Eve party at our house. People arrived by horse and cutter, bringing their molasses cakes and egg sandwiches, their guitars and fiddle and mouth organs. As I watched Gloria play with her young son, her blue velvet dress was a luxurious contrast to the faded denims and mail-order plaids around her.

Did she miss her family across the sea? How did they celebrate Christmas? My youthful imagination was stoked by Christmas card paintings of elegant English carolers singing near a crackling fire in the hearth. Just the mental picture of it warmed me. *Sitting here in a drafty farm house on the Canadian prairies, was Gloria lonesome for Christmas in her homeland?*

As if in answer to my thoughts, Gloria announced that she would like to sing a carol, but first she wanted a cup of tea with lemon to clear her throat. *Lemons in December? We hardly ever saw one in July!* There was a titter of laughter at such an unusual request, followed by an awkward silence while she sipped her plain black tea. Then, as high and clear as an angel, she began to sing, "O holy night, the stars are brightly shining; it is the night of our dear Savior's birth. . . ."

As naive and culturally deprived as we were, we did not recognize a coloratura soprano when we heard one, and we heard one that night. When the last note faded, instead of the customary ovation to which she had been accustomed in the concert halls of England, there was only limp applause; this was all but drowned by the twang of guitars and fiddles tuning up for "Turkey in the Straw."

At that moment, I think I knew that Gloria would never sing in public again. She had dared to make her debut in an adopted land, and to our everlasting shame, we did not recognize her gift.

I think of her every year at Christmas time. She was a talented woman of English opera thrust into the culturally impoverished Canadian prairies. Mocked, misunderstood, rejected, she could not hide the pain and sorrow reflected by her tears on that Christmas Eve so long ago.

Little did I realize the impact her song would have on my life. Whenever I hear "O Holy Night," I realize anew the magnificent message proclaimed by the angels on that very first Christmas, and to our everlasting shame, the awful ignorance with which we so often reject the Gift.

—*Alma Barkman*

A Stepfather's First Christmas

*I pray that God, the source of hope, will fill you completely
with joy and peace because you trust in him. Then you will
overflow with confident hope through the power of the Holy
Spirit.*
ROMANS 15:13

When I married my husband, Tom, Christmas was just
around the corner. He had come into the marriage without a family of his own, but I never doubted his ability to be a good father to my four children. However,
as the holiday season approached, there were a few
moments when I wondered how the differences in the
way we had been raised might influence his perspective on
Christmas.

Tom came from a family of ten children. Although his
father worked hard, there was little money to spare for luxu-
ries, a deficit that was keenly felt around the holidays. On
the other hand, my father was a university professor, and I
had only one older brother. Christmas at our house wasn't
excessive, but it certainly retained an air of style and pros-
perity.

During a discussion prior to our first Christmas, I
asked Tom if his family had ever observed any special tra-

ditions. He paused for a moment. "I suppose we had a few," he said.

"Like what?" I said in an encouraging voice. I was impatient to compare memories.

"Let's see," he continued. "We always had a stocking, and it usually had some socks, or oranges."

"That's all?" I said in mild disbelief.

"Well," he replied, "You have to remember there were ten of us, but everyone got new clothes. I usually got a pair of jeans and a shirt." As I listened, I realized I had lost my eagerness to share my own experiences. The cautious, thrifty ways of his large family were a sharp contrast to my memories of overflowing stockings and a mountain of presents overwhelming the tree.

Tom and I continued to reminisce, and my earlier concerns faded as I began to understand something very important. Our Christmas recollections couldn't have been more different, and yet, we had a surprising number of things in common. It wasn't what went into the stockings or how many gifts were under the tree that created the feeling of kinship that emerged that day.

Our common ground came from the love in our voices as we talked about our families and the smiles on our faces as we recalled the bittersweet moments from long ago. It came from the sense of belonging we had experienced with our families.

Most importantly, it came from the feelings of joy and peace we had received over the years from celebrating the birth of our Savior as the most important tradition of all.

It's love and togetherness that create the most cherished Christmas memories.

—*Susan B. Townsend*

PART TWO

CHRISTMAS DAY

INTRODUCTION

Jesus has a special place in His heart for children. The Bible tells us that he welcomed the little ones even as His disciples tried to keep them at a distance. In Mark 15:10, Jesus said, "I tell you the truth, anyone who doesn't receive the Kingdom of God like a child will never enter it."

Christ knew that children have an innocent, trusting view of their world, and when it comes to Christmas, they are the ones filled with hope and the steadfast belief that anything is possible on that miraculous day. Even though parents do their best to create a Christ-centered Christmas for their children, far too many adults suffer from the cynicism of the commercialized Christmas season and invariably find themselves exhausted from the obligations of the holidays.

Perhaps Christmas is the time to take the Lord's words to heart. Maybe we should search for the child within us, rediscover the wonder of the season, and return to the time when Christmas meant more than opening gifts, eating too much, and attending a plethora of parties.

It should be a time for telling and retelling the story of our Lord's birth; a time for singing Christmas carols and thinking about the meaning of the wonderful lyrics; and above all, a time for reflection and rejoicing. We can make it a day of hope, a day when we recognize that, with God, nothing is impossible. So many things about Christmas have changed over the course of two thousand years, but with the heart of a child, it's possible to remember and celebrate the truly important things associated with the day when our Lord came to earth to save the world from sin.

December 25
Prayer by the Sea

I love the sea! No earthly pleasure brings me more contentment than walking by the ocean. I am here on Christmas morning, as I have been on many Christmas mornings in the past. After the sweet hustle and bustle of Christmas shopping, opening presents with grandchildren, and eating too much of my neighbor's fudge, it is a quiet reprieve to come to my favorite spot on the beach. Few tourists break the solitude of my walk this time of year. The beach belongs to me, the birds, and God.

I marvel at the awesome majesty of God as he prompts each wave to collapse and rush to shore. I am amazed at the predictable rhythm of the tides because they are as constant as the faithfulness of God. The soothing morning sun swaddles me like a soft, cotton baby blanket and comforts my weary soul. I yield to the gentle massage of the breeze as I distinctly hear the voice of God calling me to pray. So much to pray about. So much to thank God for.

My mind reflects back to the changes over this past year. I am filled with sadness because Christmas will never be the same for two of my dearest friends. Ann lost her husband of forty-five years to a long, debilitating battle with MS. Prepared? Yes. Ready to let him go? No! Sarah was forced to say goodbye to her extremely healthy husband when he succumbed to a sudden onset of cancer. Prepared? Yes. Ready to let him go? Never!

The "firsts" after the death of a mate are met with fear and even anger: the first birthday, the first anniversary, and the first Christmas. Severe grief and loneliness shroud these times like fog hovering over the immense ocean—a fog so dense that any hope of it ever lifting is inconceivable. My need to pray for my friends this morning intensifies until I intercede for their tremendous loss. I pray they will find courage to begin new Christmas traditions while tenderly letting go of those that can never be relived. I pray that their tears of parting will flow alongside fresh tears of joy. They have a need for both tears of loss to validate their emptiness, and tears of joy to affirm the comforting presence of Christ.

I believe shattered hearts will find a way to peace and restoration when prayers go up for them. That is why I must pray. Ann and Sarah's new path will be unfamiliar and frightening. However, as I lift my face, I see the enormous span of water at my side. Its presence reminds me that I can trust my friends to God who spoke this powerful ocean into existence.

As I continue my morning walk, the seagulls fascinate me. Their sleek and brilliant white bellies fly low over my head. Spotting my small goody-bag, they seem to squawk, "What's for breakfast?"

"How about shrimp tails and fries left over from last night's dinner or perhaps a stale donut from yesterday's breakfast?" I reply. I appease their hunger by tossing them a sample of both.

Further down the beach, I spot the handle of a faded plastic shovel half-covered and crusted with sand, probably left behind by a child lathered in sunscreen. I think back many years to the joy my own children brought me when we came to this same beach. An instant replay of flying kites, slurping purple snow cones, and renting dune buggies flashes through my mind.

This Christmas morning, I sense a strong need to petition God for my daughters, their dear husbands, and my four sweet grandchildren. Please God, may they crave fellowship with other believers their age. Give them a hunger and thirst for your word and your church. Give them the courage and wisdom to bend the hearts and wills of their children toward you.

Oh yes, God, my grandchildren! Provide teachers and friends who will mold and influence their character toward you. I pray for the day each of my grandchildren decides to make you Lord and Savior of their life. I plead for your protection over them. Dear Father, open their eyes to the perfect plans you have for their lives—plans that you already have set in motion.

I look ahead toward a more remote part of the beach and a flock of seagulls gliding leisurely out to sea. I sense they know their creator more intimately than I do. Their gliding encourages me to ease my grip on life and its worries: worries about my chronically ill daughter, worries about my beloved country, and worries about the spiritual needs of people around me.

Yet, this morning I am drawn close to the heart of God and filled once again with His love. He promises that He has it all in His control, and I respond with worship and gratitude; profound gratitude much like Mary must have felt that first Christmas morning when she cradled her baby boy. I rejoice that Jesus loves me and praise God for the gift of His precious Son.

While I am still studying the gulls, an eccentric egret totters by. I wonder if he is jealous of the seagulls' agile antics as they plunge into the salty water in search of food. I smile as I spy a pelican bobbing up and down in the distant waves. Perhaps he is contemplating his own clumsiness at fishing and secretly wishing that his Creator had not demonstrated His sense by giving him such a saggy baggy bill.

Watching these wonderful sea birds gives me a photo album filled with snapshots of God's delightful creativity. Breathing in the crisp air gives me a sense of God's refreshing grace. His grace prompts me to humbly thank Him for His incredible blessings, blessings that I hope I will never take for granted: my faithful husband, the home I have loved for thirty-five years, neighbors who joke with me, Christian friends who pray with me, and, of course, two healthy legs to walk on. I linger a little longer on the beach because I have no agenda on this blessed Christmas morning—except to walk and pray.

—*Linda Blaine Powell*

The Ultimate Gift

He has removed our sins as far from us as the east is from the west.
PSALM 103:12

My brother ordered my sisters and me to be quiet, and even though Mom and Dad were away, we still used caution. On tiptoes, we sneaked down the hall. The four of us looked like thieves, and in a sense, we were.

"There," my brother said, "grab that bag." My sisters obeyed my brother's command and reached up to the top shelf of a spare closet. They pulled down a large, black garbage bag. I was too small to help, so I stood and watched. "This is it," he said. "Let's be quick before they come back." Our eyes twinkled in delight as the bag fell open and out tumbled the wrapped packages.

Yes, we did what all little kids dream of doing—we found our hidden Christmas gifts, opened them, played with them, then rewrapped and replaced them, all without our parents knowledge. Or so we thought. Our parents didn't say anything until years later when we recalled what we had done. "Oh, yes, we knew," Mom said.

"What? You knew, and we didn't get punished?" My siblings and I laughed in disbelief.

"We thought we'd get a licking," someone said.

"We decided to let it go in the hope that someone would confess," Dad replied. "As I recall, one of you did. You were curious kids. We should have hidden the gifts better. Actually, from that Christmas on, we did."

"Yeah, I know," I replied. "I couldn't find another gift after that."

Dad chuckled. "Good. That's how it's supposed to be."

Just like a parent, God sees our foolishness. The things we do in immaturity, ignorance, and oblivion. He also recognizes our intentional sins. Those deliberate times we go against His will. My brother, two sisters, and I should have been grounded for our intended disobedience.

Bad decisions often lead to physical consequences, but not always eternal consequences. Not if we have put our faith in Jesus, who loves us enough to have given His life as a ransom for all who may believe.

If you have faith in the Lord, rest assured you have been forgiven, as far as the east is from the west, of all your sins—even those indiscretions carried out as a foolish, young child. Now, that's a real Christmas gift.

Forgiveness may be for the saved; but salvation in Christ is offered to all.

—L. A. Lindburg

PART THREE

THE TWELVE DAYS
OF CHRISTMAS

INTRODUCTION

In our modern culture, "The Twelve Days of Christmas" is usually associated with the popular song that many people recall trying to memorize—with varying degrees of success—for school Christmas pageants. Yet, for hundreds of years, countless believers have marked the "The Twelve Days of Christmas" as the period beginning on December 25 and ending on January 5. The evening of December 25 is celebrated as "First Night," with the evening of January 5 distinguished as "Twelfth Night." These days are followed by Epiphany on January 6—for many Christians, the day traditionally associated with the arrival of the three Magi.

Over the centuries, a variety of different cultures, churches, and sects of Christianity established traditions for these twelve days. In America, many of these traditions were replaced with contemporary practices such as New Year's Eve parties, and in more recent times, after-Christmas sales.

However, there are still Christians who commemorate the period following Christmas with a combination of popular customs and church-led observances. Some celebrants give a gift for each of the twelve days, while others consider "Twelfth Night" as the time for parties and gift giving. Many believers light a candle each day or light a Yule log on "First Night." The log is then allowed to burn a bit each night until "Twelfth Night." Some people sing a verse of the popular song every day, and others serve traditional food. Still others observe "Twelfth Night" as the time to take down the Christmas tree and decorations.

Because many of the traditions associated with this period involve gifts, the wonderful stories that follow all have one thing in common. A few of the stories are lighthearted while others are more serious in nature, but each one involves a gift of some kind. These range from the traditional and commercial to the unexpected and spiritual. The gifts may vary, but the conclusion of the stories rarely differs. The greatest gift of all came from God on the day His Son was born.

December 26
The Lopsided Poinsettia

In my eyes, my talented first-born sister was Colorado's best version of Rembrandt, Picasso, and Van Gogh wrapped into one glorious package—certainly the closest I would ever come to a real live genuine *artiste.*

Early on, I declared her rejects to be far better than my masterpieces, and became her number one fan. She was a perfectionist, while I frolicked through life with a classic middle-child attitude, happily creating things and feeling a smidgen of adequacy in the process, valid or not. I guess it just wasn't that important to me, unless it was destined to be a special gift for someone. Those simply had to be perfect.

With Christmas waiting in the wings one year, I was bubbling over with excitement. My favorite Girl Scout activity was nearly upon us as well—our annual visit to the Denver Convalescent Home. Each year we started early, planning and preparing for an enjoyable night of Christmas caroling, and giving away the gifts we had made.

I dubbed this particular Christmas, "The Year of the Poinsettia." Troop 362 seemed to outdo itself this year, laboring for hours, crafting our floral wonders out of crimson-red crepe paper, flowerpots, colored foil, sphagnum moss, wires, and ribbons. Our collective result was supposed to be an array of beautiful poinsettia-looking plants to present to the folks at the home. I don't know about the other fifty-one girls in our troop, but I grew up knowing my renditions were probably going to be the objects of somebody's best guess.

"Oh look, our little Sandi has sculpted a rooster out of clay."

"No, dear, I think it's a buffalo, or maybe a dump truck."

Some tried hard to marvel at my efforts, and cheer me on. "Wow, honey, that sure is a lovely umm . . . an amazing-looking . . . uhh . . . well, it sure is . . . clay!"

Which brings us back to the poinsettia. Perhaps now you have a better idea of the enormity of my challenge—to create the *magnum opus* my heart desired with the limitations my hands and fingers possessed. Every chance I got, I worked on it. Meticulously molding and gluing and tending to every detail of the project, I finally put the finishing touches on my poinsettia one evening. With a great sense of accomplishment and satisfaction for a ten-year-old, I felt like announcing my success to the world and hearing them shout back, "Wow, our little Sandi managed to create the *perfect gift* for someone special—*it's a poinsettia!*" I could hardly wait to give it away on Saturday night.

Clutching our decorative pots, we cheerfully entered the convalescent home. I remembered residents from the previous year, and some of them recognized us. I didn't understand back then why our visits seemed so special to the folks in that place. Even when we messed up some of the lyrics, or sang off-key, they still liked us. Now I know why. As someone once said, children are an antidote to sadness.

Some of us in the Girl Scout troop believed that our job in life was to dispel sadness and "entertain the troops," so to speak, wherever we were "stationed." God had created us that way, and we loved it. Growing up as the resident clown and storyteller around our kitchen table, I found it highly gratifying to make people happy. So, in some ways, I suppose a trip to this place was like coming home. We made them smile, and they did the same for us.

On the way to the convalescent home, people stared at the Girl Scout uniforms we wore. I was thrilled and tried to imagine a few of the comments onlookers were making. "Look mommy, that girl has badges going all the way up the back." I never actually heard the words, but I liked to think that all our hard work was not going unnoticed in the public square. With fifty-two girls in our troop, we were a giant mass of green everywhere we went. Tonight was no exception, and our red poinsettias completed the Christmas palette beautifully. What a blessing this night would be!

Moving from room to room, poinsettias in hand, we caroled our hearts out. As we made our way through the building, I searched for that special someone. *Who needed my gift most?* Rounding the corner, we made our way in and out of some more rooms, singing, and hand-delivering more gifts along the way.

When we arrived at the doorway at the end of the hall, singing the first strains of "Joy to the World," I spotted an elderly woman over in the far corner bed. She looked sad and alone, and my heart melted. "She's the one who needs my poinsettia," I determined silently, and made my way across the room.

I held my gift out to her and started to say, "Merry Christmas," but when I looked down, I realized my poinsettia was flawed. One leaf was coming loose, and the plant lay noticeably lopsided in its pot.

Oh no, this would never do! Quickly, I started to pull it back, but it was too late. Her dim eyes had brightened when they spotted my gift; her mouth quivered into a smile as her frail, trembling hands reached out to take the foil-covered flower pot. Tears trickled down her cheeks. Our eyes met, we grinned, and for a few precious moments, we spoke volumes without a word.

I put the poinsettia where she could see it. She carefully studied it, top to bottom, flaws and all, and her obvious delight warmed my heart. I can still see her smiling from the inside out. Suddenly the words *flawed* and *lopsided* didn't seem so bad somehow. I had made that sad lady happy with my less than perfect gift.

I rejoined the group for the final stanza: ". . . And repeat, repeat, the sounding joy!" It was a night I will never forget—the imperfect gift, the joyful receiver.

Now, with a sense of awe, I reflect on that *first* Christmas night, over 2,000 years ago, when God gave His *perfect* gift to us: the Baby in the manger, the Savior of mankind. We live in a world where "buy-one-get-one-of-equal-or-lesser-value" reigns supreme, and we tend to wrestle with the very idea. How could God incarnate give His *perfect* life, in exchange for our *flawed* and sinful ones? In all these years, that kind of love remains a mystery to me. I suppose it always will.

With grandchildren, grandnieces, and grandnephews of my own, I wonder how each of them will process this gripping truth, this message of hope from John 3:16.

"For God loved the world so much that he gave his one and only Son, so that everyone who believes in him will not perish but have eternal life."

Will they embrace it, and if they do, will they pass it on to *their* children? Will they be compelled to proclaim it from the rooftops and whisper it into the heart of a dying soul? I pray so, and whenever Christmas comes around each year, filled with whirlwind activity and the temptation to dive into colorfully wrapped packages without so much as a glance at the Babe in the manger, I hope they "get it."

Christmas *is* the season of giving, but it's more than that. It's looking up into the face of our Savior and with a thankful heart seeing *His* gift as the *ultimate* Gift, and then reaching out to receive it with joy. This Christmas, may we all be generous givers—and grateful receivers!

—Sandi L. Banks

The Passage of Time

Your children and your crops
will be blessed.

The offspring of your herds and flocks
will be blessed.
DEUTERONOMY 28:4

I slid into the passenger seat of our car for the forty-minute drive to my sister's home in Pliny, West Virginia. For nearly fifty years, my husband, Ted, and I had made this trip to her home for Christmas dinner. Spending a special holiday on the farm with my sister and her husband had been a joyous occasion for everyone, but this year, it would be different. The Lord had called both of them home, and they were buried in a nearby cemetery beside the church where they had been active members all their married life. It had been a shock to all of us.

I dreaded the trip because it wouldn't be the same without my sister and her husband. Yet, in my heart, I was thankful that my nephew, Steve, and his wife, Jenny, had moved into the homestead and continued what their parents had started. Christmas dinner for our family would still be at Pliny each year.

As our car entered the gates to the farm, we could see the house sitting on a hill at the end of a long driveway. A feeling of gratitude to my Lord brightened my soul. Cows still grazed on the hill above the house, goats, pigs, and geese were all over the place, and the barn was filled with farm equipment, and barn cats. The homestead was warm and comfortable, and it smelled of ham and sweet potatoes when we walked in. Laughter from other family members already there filled the air.

However, this year, Steve stood in the doorway to greet us—in the very same spot his dad had stood for so many years before. Later, at dinner, it was Steve who asked God's blessings before we plunged into our plates of goodies. I couldn't help but ponder the passage of time and how, as King Solomon wrote, "One generation passes away, and another generation comes; but the earth abides forever." (Ecclesiastes 1:4)

Within our family, one generation had moved on and another one had taken its place. The homestead was still filled with warmth and happiness, and I knew God's presence would abide for all time. We had experienced a miracle. Our family was still strong, secure, and intact. For this precious gift, we praised the Lord.

Cherish every moment today with your family.

—*Evelyn Rhodes Smith*

December 27
The Jelly Jar

As a little girl in Sunday school class, I was always impressed by the Bible story of the widow. I could vividly imagine the poor woman in her ragged clothes clutching her only coins. In my mind's eye I saw her trying to avoid the rich people because she was embarrassed to have so little to give. Perhaps she quietly slipped her small contribution into the collection box, hoping no one would notice.

This memorable parable helped me recall another story, one told by my mother several years ago. My mother lived in another state, so I wasn't able to see her as often as I wanted. On one of my visits, I couldn't help but notice Mama's meager surroundings. Mismatched furniture crowded the room. The sofa, meant to be a maroon and green flower garden pattern, had become faded and drab. A worn storage chest held a few beloved plants and substituted as a table for visiting great grandkids to spread out their games and books to play. An ancient desk with an upper cabinet was covered with so many gouges and scratches that Goodwill would probably have rejected it. Mama didn't own many worldly possessions.

After dinner, Mama opened the doors of the desk cupboard and took out a small glass jar. The top of the jar had a rim, indicating that, at one time, there must have been a lid. The squat jar appeared quite ordinary, about three inches tall with diamond-shaped designs cut into the rounded sides.

"I think this is a jelly jar," Mama said as she cupped the jar lovingly in her hands, walked slowly to the sofa, and sat down. I knew she was about to tell me an important story.

"An old man gave the jelly jar to me when I was eight years old," Mama said. She thought for a second. "That would have been about 1913. My parents lived near the railroad tracks and one day a drifter, or what they called a hobo, wandered to our house. The old-timer begged my parents to take him in. Times were hard, and the man said he had no family, no food, and no money. He leaned on a stick he used for a cane. All he had with him was a bundle of clothes stuffed in a dirty onion sack. Our small house was already crowded with four kids, but my parents didn't have the heart to turn away the old man."

Mama paused, turned the simple jar in her hands, and gazed at it like she held a treasured jewel. She went on with her story. "As you know, my father worked as a blacksmith. His shop was in a barn in back of our house. Dad fixed a place for the drifter to sleep in his blacksmith shop. The man, who said his name was Dan Works, appeared ill. In fact, he kind of scared us kids. His wrinkled skin sagged, he walked with a limp, and he was dirty."

By this time, I was mesmerized by a story I had never heard before. Mama went on. "Once the man got settled, he showed us his sore leg. His leg was a dreadful sight—swollen and festered with foul-smelling gangrene. Of course, there were no antibiotics back then and no doctor in our little town. My mother used what she called her *Yankee ingenuity* and nursed him with the only treatment she knew, probably what she'd seen my father use for horses. She soaked the man's leg in warm water and diluted carbolic acid. Then she cleaned the infection the best she could and wrapped his leg with freshly laundered dishtowels. She cleansed and wrapped his leg several times a day.

"My job was to help Mother by carrying meals to Mr. Works at his place in back of the shop. One evening I took dinner out to him. He thanked me, opened his onion sack, and took out this jelly jar. He said he didn't have much to give, but he wanted at least to give me some little gift."

Mama looked at the jar again. Her expression spoke of the bittersweet memories she must have been feeling. "Except for a few articles of ragged clothing, this jar was all the man owned," Mama said, her voice solemn. "From a child's perspective, the jar was a wonderful gift because we kids didn't have many toys or pretty things." She breathed a heavy sigh. "Mr. Works stayed with us for several months. He finally got terribly sick so my father took him to the County Home where he died."

Mama and I sat in silence, our eyes fixed on the small glass container. I hated to interrupt the poignant moment. Finally, I murmured, "You were just a little girl. It had to be a special gift for you to save the jelly jar all these years."

"This is my reminder of what's important," she replied. "The best gifts aren't always expensive or flashy." She placed the jar in my hands and smiled. "I want you to have it."

I held the gift reverently and glanced again at Mama's apartment. Through the years my mother had kept nothing of significant value for herself. Like her parents and Mr. Works, she always gave away whatever she could to others.

It is easy to get caught up in the rush and chaos of the holiday season. When I begin to feel the pressure to purchase expensive gifts, attend meaningless parties with too much food, or send costly cards, I am reminded of the simplicity of the jelly jar.

Mama is no longer living. The jelly jar has a special place on the top shelf of my china cabinet. I enjoy taking the jar from the shelf, holding it in my hands, and recalling the beautiful story of unselfish giving. The luxury or monetary value of the gift is of no importance.

Someday I'll give the jelly jar to my daughter. I hope she will pass it on to her daughter along with the story of her generous grandmother, kind-hearted great-grandparents, and a sickly old man who showed his gratitude with a jelly jar. No one could ask for a finer inheritance or a better example of the real meaning of giving.

—*Barbara Brady*

Peace in Wartime

For a child is born to us,
a son is given to us.
The government will rest on his shoulders.
And he will be called:
Wonderful Counselor, Mighty God,
Everlasting Father, Prince of Peace.
ISAIAH 9:6

As the war in Afghanistan raged on, it became clear the Air Force wasn't about to send our son home to the States for Christmas. We worried about Dan, who e-mailed us joking that his "officer's quarters" consisted of a tent on a U.S. base in Saudi Arabia. Since my husband wrestled with his own pain over the situation, I decided to weep privately as I walked into the welcome darkness of a December night.

A few moments later, an elderly couple appeared under the glow of a streetlight. "Oh no," I thought. "It's the Murphys." Bob and Amy were family friends, who loved to chat.

As they approached, I had nowhere to run. Quickly mopping my eyes, I put on a smile and attempted to steer the conversation away from me, "Merry Christmas! How are the grandkids?"

"They're wonderful," Amy said. "How's your son? Is he coming home?"

Swallowing hard, I made a brave attempt to maintain my composure, "He's at an airbase in Saudi Arabia, fighting a war and living in a tent." Then I lost it, blurting out my worst fear: "I'm afraid some terrorist will kill him as he sleeps!"

"Oh, Honey," Amy said and gave me a comforting hug.

"Our Saudi airbase is perfectly safe," Bob said. "It's way out in the desert. No one can approach undetected. I've been there."

"You have?" I said, so stunned my tears ceased.

"Yeah!" Bob replied. "My work for the Corps of Engineers often takes me there. In fact, I just got back. Guess they like this old guy." He grinned. "They've shown me their finest places. Do you know they have gold everywhere? Saudi gold is the best."

"So, you really think Dan will be safe?" I asked.

"Absolutely!" he said and patted me on the shoulder. "When you e-mail that kid, tell him he can't come home without bringing his mother some Saudi gold." Bob winked and Amy gave me one last squeeze before they disappeared into the darkness.

As I stood alone on the sidewalk, a deep peace settled into my heart, and a supernatural confidence rose in my spirit. Dan was going to be okay. Somehow, I just knew it.

The gift of a tranquil heart comes from our "Prince of Peace"—Jesus Christ.

—*Laura L. Bradford*

December 28
No Longer a Stranger

$\mathcal{I}$t was 1968, and Christmas was going to be different. Instead of decorating, baking, and gift exchange with my family, I would spend the holidays with a family I'd never met, and in a land I'd never seen. High over the Atlantic Ocean, I tucked away the little wooden snowmen that adorned our in-flight dinner trays. They'd make a nice decoration for Christmas in the years to come.

I was accompanying Robert, the man I loved and hoped to marry, and his brother Glenn as they traveled home for Christmas. Robert's parents were missionaries in Brazil, and God had made it possible for me to travel to meet his family before Robert and I said our vows. I was grateful that Glenn had joined us at college for the past semester. He had already become my friend, and it was a comfort having another ally by my side for the coming three weeks with his parents and four other siblings.

My mind raced with thoughts of wonder and apprehension. I was flying far from home during my favorite season. What would Christmas be like in a foreign country without my family? What if I didn't like the food?

What if Robert's family didn't like me? What if we didn't get along?

As we began the descent toward Brazilia, my stomach churned with anticipation and apprehension. Robert's dad was waiting. He hugged me almost as warmly as he did his sons and gave me a souvenir demitasse spoon to welcome me. We looked through the gift shop in the airport, then boarded a small Cessna, and headed down the runway toward "home."

This was my first experience in a foreign country, my first time in a small private plane, and my first trip to meet future in-laws. I didn't want to miss a thing. I studied the ground below, taking in all I could. Even from the air the terrain looked different from anything I had been accustomed to. I knew when we neared Ceres because the ground turned red from the red clay I had heard wouldn't wash out. We dipped low and buzzed the house—a signal to the family to pick us up at the dirt landing strip.

As the plane descended briefly, I saw the roof of the house, and my mind and emotions raced. "We're here! There's the house! The family is right under that roof made of red clay tiles!" The dipping plane combined with my rising emotions created too much turbulence, and I promptly emptied the contents of my stomach into a plastic bag that Robert had thrust into my hands in the nick of time. So much for a good first impression.

There was great rejoicing as the family welcomed Robert and Glenn and graciously received me. On the way to the house, we met horse-drawn carts, bicycles, and people walking, but no cars. The dirt roads were lined with dingy zinnias, growing wild and stained gray with a thick layer of dust.

The houses were small and simple, but as we got closer to town, many of them were painted bright, cheerful colors. Some were even painted several different colors. People were everywhere. It seemed everybody was outdoors. It was all so different.

Even though it was the day before Christmas, there were no signs of the season, no decorated trees visible through open doors and windows. There were poinsettias, but they were bushes growing in yards. And they were green. They didn't bloom at this time of year.

At "home," an artificial tree brought from the United States sat in the corner of the living room. It was festooned with lights, garland, and ornaments. Christmas carols played on the record player, but it was sweltering hot. A wall surrounded the yard, and unintelligible voices of shouting children drifted through the open windows with the dust. It didn't feel like home, and it definitely didn't feel like Christmas. I tried to ignore the hollow loneliness tugging at my heart.

Someone needed one last thing from the store, so I tagged along. Even the streets in town were dirt except for one block of cobblestone downtown, and it was covered with red dirt washed down from higher ground. Open buggy taxis lined the streets. The horses that pulled them waited patiently, tails swishing furiously to swat the flies away. This time, I saw a few cars. Some people rode bicycles, but most walked.

The front metal walls on the tiny shops rolled up like garage doors. The sparse merchandise was odd and unusual, with only a few souvenirs to choose from among the basics for life. Even in the stores, there were no signs of Christmas: no trees, bells, angels, or Santas. Nothing I had seen looked like Christmas, and a twinge of homesickness crept in, threatening to smother my excitement. Surely they celebrated Christmas in Brazil.

When we got home, we ate an early supper and went to the Christmas Eve program at church. I didn't need to understand the words to follow the familiar story. First Mary and Joseph came on stage, and after being turned away by the innkeeper, they went to the stable. Little angels, with halos tilted and wings askew, appeared next to greet a small group of shepherds in the field. The shepherds rushed to worship the baby lying in a manger. Just like at home, the Wise Men brought their foil-wrapped gifts to present to the infant Jesus. Interspersed in the story were the carols I had enjoyed my whole life, sung with gusto and joy.

It was then I began to understand. Christmas meant remembering the story of the night Jesus Christ was born. It was singing carols, and people coming together at a church play to celebrate the birth of a baby who would grow up to be our Savior. It wasn't about snow, decorated trees, or decorations in stores. It didn't matter where I spent Christmas. Suddenly, it felt more like Christmas—and more like home.

As we gathered around the tree, I missed my family, but my homesickness began to fade as someone read the Christmas story from the book of Luke. I watched eagerly when Robert's four younger siblings opened the presents we had brought them. I was a stranger among them so didn't expect any gifts, but I received one present after another: a barrette, handmade just for me; Brazilian dishes, and even some money to spend on our trip to the big city the following week. I was thrilled to be treated just like one of the family.

Nothing in my environment had changed. I was still in a foreign country trying to decipher an unknown language. The dust drifting through the windows still clung to our sweaty skin, but suddenly it was Christmas. I was no longer an outsider, and I believe it came about through the gifts we had given and shared. Gifts like love and small tokens of affection and appreciation. There was no doubt in my mind or heart that I had been received as a member of the family.

In the same way, God gave us His only Son on Christmas Day. Thanks to His miraculous gift, we can become part of God's family. Jesus made it possible for us to be reconciled to God, and that's what Christmas is about.

—*Kay W. Camenisch*

A Wonderful Life

Yet God has made everything beautiful for its own time.
He has planted eternity in the human heart, but even so,
people cannot see the whole scope of God's work from
beginning to end.
ECCLESIASTES 3:11

December arrived with a whimper and a sob at the end of
a year that had brought enough grief to fill Santa Claus's
bag. Most of all, I dreaded my first Christmas without my
daughter, who had died in March. That fall, my mother
underwent heart surgery, and I had a total knee replacement. On top of that, my employer canceled my vacation
to see my son's family.

Mom and I didn't put up a tree, bake cookies, or wrap
presents. We did watch a number of wonderful holiday
movies. Frank Capra's classic, *It's a Wonderful Life*, was
an annual favorite, and as I followed the familiar story, I
identified with George Bailey more than ever. Similar to
George, I felt I had traded my dreams for futility; but unlike
Jimmy Stewart's character, I didn't believe I had touched
anyone's life.

In the movie, God sends a wannabe angel named
Clarence to straighten out George Bailey's pessimistic out-
look. God knew I also needed an attitude adjustment, but

instead of a trainee angel, he brought an old friend back into my life. I hadn't seen Linda in almost thirty years. We had been best friends in childhood, until time and multiple moves separated us. On my twelfth birthday, I shared the plan of salvation with her, and she prayed to receive Christ. Years passed, and I wondered if Linda's salvation experience had been genuine. Perhaps she had felt pressed to "join the club" because of our friendship.

In an e-mail, Linda confessed that she had strayed from God. Her father died, and she survived breast cancer. She said, "On a gray day, I thought of how my life had turned into a real mess and how impossible it was for me to run it. Then I remembered the 'C, B, A,' you explained to me: confess, believe, and ask. I repeated the prayer you taught me, and I came back to the Lord."

In my reunion with Linda, God helped me see a glimpse of the beautiful work He was creating out of my life, instead of the failures I perceived.

That was a gift to treasure on Christmas morning and always.

From God's viewpoint, I have a wonderful life.

—*Darlene Franklin*

December 29

Kindred Souls

I expected to spread Christmas cheer one night. I didn't expect to receive it. The winter sky was clear, the night air cold. The sound of snow crunching under our feet seemed to freeze in midair as we walked up the sidewalk toward the nursing home.

My husband took hold of my arm and held it tightly, partly to steady my step and partly to keep me from turning around to go back to the car. We were headed down a path I was not prepared to go, and he knew it.

I was the first of our little troupe of carolers to step inside the nursing home doors, so I went to the front desk to get the room numbers of the individuals our group had been assigned to carol. As I handed the desk attendant the index card on which the names were listed, I glanced tentatively over my shoulder.

There he was, sitting alone in his wheelchair, staring straight out the window into the star-filled December sky. His profile was distinct. I knew it was him. I wanted to walk toward him; yet, I held back, frozen in place like the remains of last summer's flowers in the garden outside the nursing home entrance. Why hadn't my husband given me more notice that our group had been assigned to spread Christmas cheer at this particular nursing home? I could have prepared myself to face that which I had been avoiding for several months—a reunion with a lifelong friend.

My emotions whirled out of control in multiple directions like wisps of snow caught by a sudden gust of prairie wind. Stay. Flee. Approach. Withdraw. Acknowledge. Ignore. Seize the moment. Waste the opportunity. Smile. Cry. We had shared so much once, starting in the era of black and white television: holiday dinners, evenings watching presidential election returns, church services, birthday parties, and Sunday School birthday offerings. We had the same birth date, but he was older—by three dozen years, to be exact. The year he dropped forty-eight pennies in the special Sunday school birthday offering plate, I dropped in twelve.

He, his wife, and their two sons always set aside one evening during the Christmas holiday season to get together with my parents, my sister, and me. Seeing him, motionless and aged by time and illness, I gathered the memories of all those Christmases past and tried to put them in a safe place. If only I could gather them all up, put them in a box covered with shiny paper, and secure them with a silver cord. Then, I would be able to keep them forever.

I could pull the box from the corner of my mind and peek inside at souvenir memories from the days when my life was simpler, when everyone I loved lived close by, and when I wasn't keenly aware of the cold reality that I might be celebrating Christmas with a friend for the last time.

I tugged on the silver cord of my memory box, making sure no treasured memories could escape, and I walked the long journey of a few steps to where "Mush-mush" was sitting in his wheelchair. "Mush-mush" was the name I had given him when I was very young and we had exchanged mutual birthday hugs and kisses. I pulled one of the nearby reception area chairs over next to his wheelchair and sat down beside him.

"Hi, Mush-mush," I said, choking back tears. He turned and looked at me. When he did, I saw Christmas. I didn't see it in the strings of colored lights on the nursing home's tree. I didn't see it in the wonder-filled eyes of the children in our caroling group. I saw Christmas in the eyes of my friend. While my fellow carolers sang, his eyes were fixed in a forward stare, as if he was all alone in the room. Still, there was that one precious fleeting moment when he turned and looked at me. Our eyes met and his soul once again touched mine—and I saw Christmas.

I wrapped my arms around his shoulders and told him I loved him. Numerous strokes had made speech difficult for him, but with much deliberate effort, he was able to say, "I love you, too." When he did, I heard Christmas. I didn't hear it in the familiar carols being sung by my friends or in the distant ringing of church steeple bells. My friend told me he loved me, and I heard Christmas.

I felt Christmas as I held my friend's hands. Once strong and worn by decades of farm life, they were now soft and fragile and lay folded in his lap. I had expected to feel Christmas in the chill of the crisp winter air as we traveled from one caroling assignment to another. I cradled my friend's hands in mine, and our kindred souls were transported to shared memories of Christmas. And I felt Christmas.

Tears spilled onto Mush-mush's cheeks as we presented the Christmas message in song. I expected to taste Christmas in candy canes, homemade fudge and cookies, or in the hot chocolate and warm, spiced apple cider after we were finished caroling and gathered with other groups back at our church. I didn't expect to taste Christmas in my friend's tears, but as I kissed his moistened cheek, I did.

Then, as quickly as our eyes had met and our souls had touched, the connection was broken. My friend's dim mind, like an evening star just before the sun overpowers it, could no longer grasp all I was trying to say to him. His gaze was once again fixed on some other place, and perhaps, some other time.

The tears continued to roll down his cheeks, and I knew he had experienced Christmas too. He had seen it, heard it, and felt it. He was a godly man, and God had given him a special gift—the gift of rekindled flames of Christmas joy in his heart. It was a testimony to the power of the Christmas message to transcend all limitations of the physical body.

In the amount of time it took our small group of carolers to sing three familiar Christmas songs, a miracle occurred. The silver cord of my memory box had been loosened, and a new, very precious Christmas memory was placed safely inside.

I expected to spread Christmas cheer last night, but I didn't expect to receive it in the all-too-brief company of an elderly lifelong friend. I expected to spread Christmas cheer last night, but instead it was given to me.

—*Valerie Kay Gwin*

A Sweet Gift

*They entered the house and saw the child with his mother,
Mary, and they bowed down and worshiped him. Then
they opened their treasure chests and gave him gifts of gold,
frankincense, and myrrh.*
MATTHEW 2:11

The church was packed. Parents and grandparents, jittery with anticipation, lined the back of the auditorium with cameras at the ready. The children were presenting a program titled "The A to Z's of Christmas."

The program director urged each small child to the center of the platform to present his or her letter. "A" is for the angel who announced Jesus' birth. "B" is for baby Jesus born in a stable." And on it went without a hitch—until the letter "F."

A precious boy about four years old marched to the center of the stage, and stepped forward. With a booming voice he shouted into the microphone, "'F' is for frankensniff."

Although the crowd laughed at his mispronunciation, the young man wasn't altogether mistaken. Frankincense is a gum resin that burns with a clear white flame and gives off a fragrant balsam-like odor. It was used as one of the ingredients in the perfume of the sanctuary as a symbol of prayer, and while it was offered, the people prayed and their prayers ascended with the sweet odor of the incense.

When the Magi came to see the Christ Child, they carried treasure worthy for the King of Kings. They brought the gift of frankincense to the holy child in Bethlehem as a symbol of His sacrifice and heavenly role as our eternal high priest. God gave His best, His only Son, Jesus Christ, as a sacrifice for us.

Even though the little guy in the program didn't say his word correctly, his chest puffed out as he gave his best performance. As a child of God, I want to do the same—give my best as an offering to the Lord and worship Jesus as my Savior and King.

We should strive to be living sacrifices, a sweet-smelling savor to God.

—*Donna J. Shepherd*

December 30
Secret Socks

"Bingo!" A family member yelled in delight. The Christmas tradition of gift exchange via competition was well underway. I sat next to Aunt Judy and bounced my youngest child on my knee. For years, the family had drawn names as a means of gift giving at Christmas. That practice ended the Christmas before, and now we played bingo. Gifts were brought by every family member to ensure enough presents were provided. Many brought more than one, so some players received two or three gifts.

Everyone sat around the kitchen and listened for the next call numbers. Aunts, uncles, cousins, nieces, and nephews huddled at small card tables, big bench tables, on the couches, and on the floor. Red and white bingo play cards sprinkled the area.

Aunt Judy enjoyed bingo play, but unlike the other participants, her real pleasure came from seeing others yell "bingo" and grab a gift. She had bowed out from a win on occasion just to watch the family play. Her gracious heart had touched many, including me. She and her husband's merciful hands had reached out to help my little family of four more than once. Little did I know God would provide an opportunity for me to give in return.

My lucky husband, Tim, raked in all the cool gifts—cash, gift certificates, and sports stuff. With a one-year-old child on my lap, I picked up more game pieces off the floor than I put on my card. Only a couple of items decorated my spot at the table: a green plaid scarf and a small Lego set. Aunt Judy marked my card with a red M&M while I wrestled with my son who insisted on eating all the place markers.

"Bingo!" Tim's younger cousin Lacy yelled as she jumped up from the bench. She occupied the seat opposite me on the other side of Aunt Judy. Lacy skipped to the gift table and chose her package. Back at our table, she pulled away the tissue paper to reveal a pair of fuzzy socks: black and white print with grips on the bottom.

"Oh, those are nice," Aunt Judy said. She reached over and felt the velvety texture. Her eyes danced over the detail of the snowflake design. "Lacy, would you like to trade?"

Lacy scanned the items Aunt Judy had won. "No thanks."

"Now you wouldn't want my feet to get cold at night," Aunt Judy continued in a more determined voice. "Just think of my chilly house in the country. Please, Lacy. Have sympathy on you poor Aunty."

As I listened to the exchange, I couldn't be certain of Aunt Judy's motivation. Was she just teasing Lacy, or did she really want to possess those fuzzy socks?

Lacy contemplated the offer once more. "Sorry, Aunt Judy, but I really want to keep the socks." Lacy turned to her cousin and the two girls began to talk and giggle.

Throughout the evening, uncles, cousins, and grandparents continued to yell "bingo!" and pick a present. Nothing perked my interest until Tim won again, and I heard Lacy comment on his prize selection. "He got the one I wanted," she said in a whiny voice. "Mom brought those gift cards, but wouldn't tell me which package she put them in. And I almost picked that one, too."

I grinned. Lacy's dilemma had just solved my problem. When the Christmas festivities ended, all the family members pitched in to clean up. In no time, the bingo game, tables, chairs, and scattered wrapping paper were in their proper places. Tim and I said our goodbyes and hauled our sleepy boys into the cold, winter night.

On the way out to the car, my plan took shape. "Tim, Aunt Judy really wanted a pair of socks tonight. I know the person who has them, and I also know they would like the gift certificate you won. Would you let me exchange the card for the socks and give them to Aunt Judy?"

Tim sighed. "I do like that restaurant. Great burgers. But I suppose you can trade," he said and handed me the envelope. I thanked him with a big kiss then ran back toward the house.

I found Lacy sitting beside her dad on the couch. I plopped myself down next to her, and when I saw Aunt Judy with her sisters in the kitchen, I gave Lacy a gentle nudge and struck my deal. "Hey, would you trade those fuzzy socks for a gift certificate?" I showed her the envelope with the restaurant logo. Without hesitation, Lacy answered. "Yes. Are you sure? I mean, the socks aren't worth as much."

"I know, but I really want the socks. I have a friend who would like them."

"Okay, if you say so." We swapped items and said good-bye.

I believed I had escaped unnoticed until I heard Aunt Judy's voice just as I opened the door to leave. "Did you forget something?"

Sweat droplets formed on my temples. I felt like a soldier caught in enemy territory.

"Yes, I needed to ask someone a question." I forced a laugh. "Got what I needed. Have a good night." I nodded and turned to leave.

Aunt Judy smiled and waved. Then she told Uncle George it was time for them to leave as well.

"I've got to go," I thought, and slipped out the door. I hurried to my car where an empty Christmas gift bag sat on the passenger floor.

Tim watched with interest. "What are you doing now?"

"Wait and see," I answered without a glance in his direction. I placed the socks in the bag and fluffed the tissue paper. "Where is Aunt Judy's car?" I asked. Tim pointed to the white sedan next to the curb. "Be right back," I said and I crept along like a ninja, all the time watching the house so as not to be seen. I grabbed the car door handle and jiggled it. Was it locked? I tried the handle again, and the door opened.

I set the gift on the passenger seat and left a note. "Thanks for everything you've done. Merry Christmas!" I scurried back to Tim, and as we pulled away, I watched Aunt Judy and Uncle George emerge from the house. I smiled—my mission accomplished.

At my in-laws, Tim and I bathed the boys and put them down for the night. By the time we finished, my father-in-law had returned from the bingo party. He called for us to join him in the kitchen. "Here," he said and handed Tim a folded bill. "Someone at the party, who wishes to remain anonymous, wanted you two to have this. They said they remember Christmas with little kids and how tight the purse strings can be."

Tim's eyes widened as he unfolded the bill to reveal fifty dollars. "Wow," he said.

My eyes filled with tears, and a few moments went by before I could speak. "Please give them our thanks."

Aunt Judy never mentioned the secret socks, and I will probably never know who gave us the money, but my heart still overflows with joy.

Just as scripture promises us, God rewards the humble giver, perhaps with fifty dollars or an overwhelming sense of peace and love. Either way, the giver never departs empty handed.

—*L. A. Lindburgh*

Taken for Granted

Ears to hear and eyes to see—both are gifts from the Lord.
PROVERBS 20:12

A week before Christmas, I happened to be driving by my friend's apartment, so I stopped to see if she needed anything. Pam had recently tripped and broken her arm. Now, it was in a cast, which made even small tasks difficult.

"Could you open some cans for me?" She set an opener on the kitchen counter, and I removed the lids. Pam dumped the salmon into a bowl and said, "That should keep me going for a few days."

My heart sank. I felt even worse when I saw her bare refrigerator.

She'd be leaving soon to spend the holidays at her daughter's home, but in the meantime, she could use some help. "Let's go out to lunch," I said.

Pam likes healthy food, so we went to a restaurant with a salad bar. I wasn't sure how she would manage. Besides a broken arm, she had been legally blind since birth, and filling her plate might be a challenge. While she's always been quick to laugh at herself, others might not be amused if she stuck her hand in the honey-mustard dressing. We decided that I would name all the choices in front of us and then put what she wanted on her plate.

We enjoyed our lunch. When we returned to her apartment, she gave me a hug, and her hearing aid made a high-pitched noise in my ear. "Don't go, yet," she said. "I've got something for you." She disappeared into the bedroom, and while I waited, I looked around. Photographs of her seven children, including twin boys, hung on the walls. Pam often said that with God's help anything can be accomplished.

A desk held the special computer that read back the words she typed. I picked up a thick book from a nearby shelf and found five of her stories in it. She wrote about her blindness, not to seek pity, but to help her readers appreciate their sight.

Pam came out of the bedroom cradling a bottle with her good arm. "Merry Christmas," she said and handed me an apothecary jar full of fragrant rose petals. Little did she know, she had already given me a wonderful present. I would never take my vision for granted again.

The perseverance of a disabled person can open your eyes to God's gifts.

—*Mary Laufer*

December 31
The Christmas of the Great Ice Storm

I was born in Northern Canada, so there were a lot of small adjustments to make when I moved to Virginia in 1998. One of the bigger disappointments came with the realization that I probably wasn't going to get the white Christmas I had grown accustomed to during my childhood. Snowfall in Virginia wasn't impossible, but it wasn't an accepted fact, either. In the weeks leading up to Christmas, I often found myself asking God if we might get a few inches to cover the beautiful countryside surrounding my home.

In a way, I suppose He did answer my prayer, but it wasn't in the form of a bit of snow. Our county was assaulted by one of the worst ice storms in the history of the area. The world

I saw when I went to bed on Christmas Eve and the world I saw when I woke up a few hours later had little in common. Christmas morning had been sealed under a thick case of ice. It was everywhere, and it had done considerable damage. The highway in front of my window, already under a sheet of ice as thick as the road itself, was a graveyard of battered tree branches and ruined power lines.

It should probably go without saying that we didn't have any electricity. Initially, the battery-powered radio didn't have much to offer in the way of help. They were still calculating the devastation. Calling the power company didn't get us anywhere, either. Every call ended with the same pre-taped message that they were aware of the damage and were doing everything possible to assess the situation and restore power as soon as possible.

My stepfather, a mysterious new figure in my life, actually worked at the nearby power station. It was his assessment, shortly before the family gathered to open presents under candlelight, that we should expect to be without power indefinitely.

It also didn't help my teenage feelings of doom and despair that almost everything I got required electricity in some way. The new video game I had wanted to play for months was easily at the top of that list. I received a wonderful cache of gifts, but nothing I could actually use with candles and the chill that saturated our ancient farm house because the heater was no longer running.

I knew I was supposed to be grateful, and I knew that what really mattered was being with my family to celebrate the birth of our Savior. However, it was difficult to keep all of that in mind while staring at a table full of amazing gifts that were going to be absolutely useless to me for the next few days or more.

Perhaps I should have been paying attention to how happy my mother was. This was her first Christmas with her new husband, my new father, and I couldn't remember the last time I had seen her enjoy Christmas so much. There was something about my stepfather that seemed to lift some of the holiday stress I had always assumed came with being a mother.

Personally, I wasn't completely sold on him. He seemed nice enough, and my mother certainly loved him, but it was hard to change gears suddenly and think of him as my father. There was never any pressure to do so, but it still seemed like a problem in my own mind. It also didn't help that I felt as though he didn't understand or care about how miserable I was that Christmas morning.

As far as he was concerned, there wasn't much we could do about the power. Instead, he told me, we should focus on the blessings we had at that moment in time. Practical advice, to be sure, but my youthful sense of greed wasn't really interested in the practical. I wanted sympathy. I wanted understanding. Most of all, I wanted something pretty close to my idea of a Christmas miracle.

The day passed slowly, as did the day after that. By the third day, everything was still the same, and my stepfather still didn't seem to be worried. I couldn't believe it. I felt like the only one who cared that Christmas had been ruined.

Then, because He had been there the whole time, God showed me just how wrong I was. It was the fourth day of the ice storm aftermath, and there still didn't seem to be an end in sight. I woke up that morning to find nothing changed, except for one small thing. I looked over at the clock on my dresser and noticed that it was blinking. I looked over at my television and realized it was on. I had to glance outside again to make sure that yes, the power lines were indeed still down. I ran downstairs and found my mother and younger siblings watching television in the playroom with my stepfather.

"We have power," I said, still mired in enough disbelief to state the obvious.

"Tom bought a generator this morning," my mother said and put a hand on my stepfather's knee.

My stepfather shrugged. "Well, we can't go crazy plugging everything in, but this should make things a little easier while we wait for the power to come back on."

I looked at my stepfather, and for the first time, I understood what my mother liked about him. He wasn't trying to win any brownie points. He was just trying to make his new family happy during the holidays. I also understood why God had taken so long in making this clear to me. He wanted me to be selfish, because He knew it would be that much more startling when I saw my stepfather for who he really was. He wanted me to give in to a moment of considering nothing but my own feelings, because he knew it would allow me to appreciate my family and being able to celebrate Christmas with them that much more.

"We're just watching *Miracle on 34th Street*," my stepfather said. "You're welcome to join us, but I imagine you'd like to go upstairs and finally play that new videogame of yours."

I turned and was on my way upstairs when I realized I didn't want to play it just yet. The game would be there as long as I wanted it to be. It could wait. What sounded much more appealing was the chance to sit down with my family and enjoy Christmas by celebrating the birth of Christ and celebrating the gift of a family I loved more than anything.

"Sounds good to me," I said and found a place on the couch.

—*Gabriel Ricard*

Making All Things New

And the one sitting on the throne said, "Look, I am making everything new!"
REVELATION 21:5

Like most children, my kids love Christmas. Around February, my youngest child starts asking, "How long until Christmas?" And why not? Christmas is wonderful, and everything is exciting. Houses and buildings glow with colorful lights and decorations, and everyone seems just a little happier. It's the days immediately following Christmas that present a problem.

As the hustle and bustle of the holiday comes to a screeching halt, my kids suddenly deflate like one of my infamous soufflés. Gifts have been opened, extended family has returned home, and decorations are hidden away in boxes. That's when the long faces appear and the postholiday doldrums set in.

A few years ago, I became determined to change this transition period of Christmas to New Year's from one of gloom and sorrow to gladness and anticipation. My first step was to involve the entire family in "un-decorating" the house. As we take down decorations, we now also take inventory of the year we're leaving behind. Instead of trying to get the house back to "normal" as quickly as possible, we take our time. We discuss the good, the bad, and the lessons learned from the previous year over hot chocolate and leftover holiday goodies.

Next, I began a tradition of reviewing our year with pictures. Each evening we watch a home movie or look through photos of vacations, events, and holidays of the past year. Finally, on New Year's Eve, we have a family time of worship and prayer. During this special time together, we thank God for the blessings He's showered upon us and pray for all He has in store for us in the upcoming year.

The after-Christmas blues have melted away as my children now eagerly look forward to the final week of the year. They love reliving the memories of what the old year held, while anticipating how God will use the lessons they learned as well as the hard times they endured for His glory during the New Year.

Never mourn for the past, because God can take the old and make it new.

—*Renee Gray-Wilburn*

January 1

John's Gift

The first time my son, John, held a crayon, he set out to create something: a cat, a dog, a tree, or a creature and place no one had ever seen before. He drew while watching television, eating at the table, and riding in the car. He drew on homework, in school and in church, as if an unseen force drove his fingers, and he couldn't stop.

At age five, he took art lessons, and on more than one occasion, his teacher told me, "He has the gift." She explained how she could teach the basics of drawing and the different techniques of painting watercolor, pastels, charcoal, acrylic, and oils. "But," she said, "a talent like John has comes from God."

She took me on a tour of her studio. "I set different models on that table and ask the students to draw what they see," she said. She showed me art her students had done: vases, bowls of fruit, a piece of driftwood. Each piece a masterpiece created by a child's hands.

"You have some talented students," I said.

She smiled. "Let me show you some of John's work."

I followed her to another stack where she picked up the top picture.

"This is John's painting of the fruit." I took the artwork and followed her as she guided me through his painting.

"Notice the detail, how he shaded the shadow of the bowl underneath and highlighted the light reflecting off the orange?" I nodded. "But look beyond the bowl."

I scanned the page, holding the curling edges taut. There was a light above the painted bowl of fruit. I glanced over at the light above the table. It was identical to the painted version, down to each tiny link in the chain holding the fixture.

"Look at this," his instructor said pointing at his painting. "My art books on the table, my paint jar, and the shelf beside the table with each item."

I looked at each and compared them on the real items. Chills of amazement ran through me. "He sees beyond the obvious," she said. "He sees the bigger picture."

She chose another of John's drawings, a fire-breathing dragon with enormous wings and a tiny figure of a man fighting the creature with his sword. Each individual scale had been drawn on the dragon and the fire exploding from its mouth and nostrils was so real, you would hesitate touching it for fear of being burned.

The ground beneath John's figures was just as complex, with different-sized stones, tiny cracks, wide crevices, and dust rising beneath the valiant man's feet. The sky revealed a bright orange sun setting behind a rocky mountain range. His teacher said, "Most artists draw from models or land-scapes they see. But John can draw this kind of detail in things he doesn't see or may have never seen. Only a select few have this gift."

Gift—there was that word again, and as I soon dis-covered, gifts can come with trials. John struggled in his school work. "He has problems paying attention," one teacher said.

"He's looking at the board, but his mind is miles away from school work," another teacher said.

"He needs to be in a special reading class," still another one said.

Then we heard other words: attention deficit disorder, medication. So, every night we read and did flash cards at the dinner table. Weekly, I took John to tutoring. Even though medication did help John concentrate and stay on task, he hated how it made him feel. We slowly worked our way through each grade.

John's best friend, Josh, was also an artist, and throughout school, they yelled and loped through the woods behind our house, imaginations running wild along with them. They drew their own superheroes and developed "save-the-world" plots. They created other worlds with powerful enemies threatening to take over the earth and its people, drawings in which the blades of grass in a meadow could easily be counted, as well as the strands of hair draping a character's shoulders. They had big plans for their artistic endeavors, and I couldn't wait.

I received a letter from John's high school telling me that John would be recognized on award's day, but no one had to tell me which award he would be receiving. I perched on the bleachers in a gym filled with loud voices and the clamor of students finding their seats. John sat in a tidy line of chairs on the floor, and I watched as he teased the girl sitting beside him, clowning around like he always did. The long program was a blur except for the art teacher stepping to the podium and calling John up to accept an award.

After the program, I went to John's art classroom to thank his teacher. "John's one of my most talented art students," he said. "He supervised our school mural project and drew most of it. Come on. I'll show you." As I followed him out of the classroom, he said, "He certainly has a gift."

When the local Museum of Art held its Youth Art Competition, John entered a few of his pieces and won "Best of Show." He also sold his first art piece—to me. After John graduated, we looked into art colleges, but there was one problem. School and John had never mixed. All he related to the word "school" were other negative words.

One day, he brought home two more words: army and infantry. He left for boot camp at Fort Benning in September 2006. I was terrified because troops were being regularly deployed to Iraq. Daily newscasts spoke of the casualty counts, and there appeared to be no end in sight for this war.

At John's graduation, he received an award for marksmanship. I was proud, but frightened. All I'd ever seen in John's hands were crayons, pencils, and paint brushes—not weapons.

From Fort Benning, he was transferred to Fort Hood. After extensive training, he was deployed to Baghdad, Iraq, to serve in a personal security detail.

Throughout my house, John's paintings and drawings hung on the walls, and I longed for his gift to bring colorful life into our life once more. Every day, I questioned the Lord and prayed about His plan for John and his gift. All I could see was that weapon in my son's hands.

The phone rang early one morning and I rushed to answer it, smiling immediately when I heard John's voice. "Hey, Mama. How's it going there?"

"Fine," I replied. "How are things there? You need anything?"

"I'm fine, Mama. Really, I am. But I do need something."

"What?"

"The kids here are always asking for soccer balls."

"Soccer balls?"

"Yeah, and there's this one kid—I call him 'Little Buddy'—who comes to the fence asking me for a ball. I'd really like to give him one. A nice one."

"I'll see what I can do."

I hung up and called my pastor immediately. "We'll send John a whole box of soccer balls," he said. The church's box filled with soccer balls, and my box filled with goodies for John and a special ball for Little Buddy. I imagined the Iraqi children crowding around John to receive their ball. Suddenly, I understood. John's gift still lay within his hands, but not with a paintbrush or a pencil. With his love for the children, he was creating something so much bigger than what he could create on paper.

I thought about God's gift to us on that starry night while the shepherds watched over their flocks. God's plan for His Son's life was so much bigger than anything Jesus' mother Mary, His friends, or even His disciples could imagine. Those people all loved and honored Jesus, but they weren't able to see past the obvious to consider the bigger picture.

Now, I know now that God's plan is so much bigger for my son and the gift that lies within John's hands. So much bigger.

—Richelle Putnam

Beginning Again

And so I tell you, keep on asking, and you will receive what you ask for. Keep on seeking, and you will find. Keep on knocking, and the door will be opened to you. For everyone who asks, receives. Everyone who seeks, finds. And to everyone who knocks, the door will be opened.
LUKE 11:9–10

The tree is down, the red bow has been removed from the mailbox, the twinkle lights are packed away, and shouts of "Happy New Year!" are fading. I'm left with a brand-new year, a new beginning with a fresh unspoiled space of time stretched out before me. I will write myself into the New Year. I will sit down and write a letter to the Lord in my journal, telling him where I am and where I want to go.

I will confess my sins of the past year, my procrastination, my waste of time, my lack of discipline, and the fact that I didn't live up to the resolutions I made last year. I will ask him to erase all that failure. I'll tell him again about my hopes and dreams and ask him to start me on a new path of becoming all I can be in this world.

I don't believe in luck, or "whatever will be, will be." I believe in work and faith and heavenly guidance. I know God has made me responsible for my own happiness. More

263

than that, I believe He has put me in my corner of the world for a purpose. He wants me to cooperate with Him in lighting a few candles that chase away the darkness.

I pray "Dear God, don't let me spoil it. Don't let me waste this brand-new year on worthless pursuits. Wake me each morning to spend the first moments with you. Give me your light and your direction for each new day. I will begin all over again each morning with you—the Master Planner of my life."

Every day is a chance to begin again with the Lord.

—*Virginia Dawkins*

January 2

A Legacy of Love

Uncle John's low, mellifluous voice filled the living room as he read from the old family Bible. I looked around the room at our family, and my gaze fell on my tiny granddaughter, Olivia, snuggled next to Rosalie. "This is so right—my two angels together on Christmas Eve," I thought and, then, I came to a decision. It was time to let Rosalie go. So, for one last Christmas, Rosalie sat like royalty at her place of honor beside our tree. Her eyes danced in the candlelight, and her half-smile never faded as she presided over our festivities.

Rosalie is our oldest family member. She is a "Parisienne," or "French Fashion," doll that has been passed down to the eldest daughter in each generation of our family for well over a century. She possesses a sophistication and dignity characteristic of a wealthy French lady of her era, which is estimated to be in the mid-1880s. Her slender body is dressed in layers of sapphire-blue taffeta, and her matching chapeau is adorned with tiny pink rosebuds. Her translucent face and arms are bisque, her body is kid, and her tiny shoes are leather.

Everything is original, except her hair, which at some point was replaced by a wig fashioned from my grandmother's own strawberry blonde tresses. Rosalie is a work of art, but she is so much more than that. She is a work of the heart—a cherished inheritance of love and family continuity.

It wouldn't be Christmas without Rosalie, and my earliest memories are rich and full because of the traditions surrounding her. Every Christmas Eve, my mother would open the cedar-lined mahogany chest where the doll was stored and bring her to our living room. There she watched over our Christmas celebration while perched on my childhood rocker beside the tree.

When she first arrived at the beginning of the holidays, she always carried the pungent scent of cedar, but within a few days, she took on the more soothing aromas of pine and holiday baking. As a small child, I sat beside Rosalie, pretending to share my cocoa and holiday cookies with her. When our family gathered around the piano to sing carols, I was certain she joined in singing praises to our Heavenly Father for His glorious gift. No matter what sadness had visited our family that year, the simple tradition of bringing out our beloved doll worked the magic of hope and renewal in our hearts.

When I was eight years old, my beloved Aunt Bab died after a long and difficult battle with cancer, and Rosalie was given to me. "This doll is very special, honey," my mother said. "She has a long and colorful history, and I'd like you to respect that. Aunt Bab cherished Rosalie and I want you to do the same."

As I held the incredible doll, unable to believe she was truly mine, my mother continued. "Rosalie is the link to the people in our family who have passed before us," she said. "We know they are safe in the arms of our Lord just as surely as Rosalie is cradled in your arms right now. They trusted in the saving power of Jesus, as you and I have, and someday we'll all be together in heaven rejoicing and praising God. What a wonderful day that will be!"

Most of the time, Rosalie remained packed away in the cedar chest, but during my times of need, I was allowed to spend time with her. To the adults in my world, Rosalie was a lovely and valuable heirloom, a symbol of family unity, but to me she was solace when I was sick and welcome company when I was lonely or frightened. She was a friend who listened without interrupting or judging. I can still see her soft brown eyes gazing at me with what I knew must be love and understanding. Of course, now I know that her faithful presence was but a mere shadow compared to that of our Lord's endless devotion.

Mother loved to share stories of her childhood, as well as those of her mother and grandmother. Details of Rosalie's "life" were often included in these sagas. One of my mother's most memorable tales described our ancestors' journey to California in a covered wagon. While fording a river, they found themselves in grave danger. The wagon began to sink, and they realized they had to lighten their load. As they prayed for God's guidance and protection, they sacrificed many valuables, including furniture and precious provisions, but they could not convince their young daughter to part with her beloved doll. After I listened to the amazing account of their harrowing experience, I couldn't help but think about God's assurance in Isaiah 43:2: "When you pass through the waters, I will be with you; and when you pass through the rivers, they will not sweep over you."

When my mother died, I clung to Rosalie for consolation. I was an adult by that time, and I know some people might consider it childish to turn to a doll for solace, but her benevolent presence, a comfort since childhood, was just what I needed in those first raw days of grief. During times of crisis and upheaval, Rosalie's presence has soothed and encouraged me. Many times through the years, with tears streaming down my face, I have traced Rosalie's tranquil features and gazed into her gentle, expressive eyes, so free from worry and sadness, and remembered God's promise to never leave me.

Rosalie was there, during the Great Depression, when my grandparents lost nearly everything. My mother told me that Rosalie's elegant appearance during those bleak years gave my grandparents hope for better days to come. She survived a horrific earthquake in the 1950s that severely damaged my childhood home, and she stayed by my side through a difficult illness when I was nine. I can still feel the coolness of her bisque face against my feverish skin. Rosalie has always survived our family's trials and triumphs with grace and dignity.

The past, present, and future of our small family are embodied in this priceless heirloom. Because I wanted to share all that Rosalie has meant to me, I decided to break with the family custom of waiting until the passing of the eldest daughter to bequeath our doll to the next generation. I am ready to relinquish Rosalie to my daughter's young family next Christmas so they can begin establishing their own traditions. What a joy it will be for me to watch Rosalie with her new family as they celebrate the birth of our Lord Jesus Christ, the *real* source of our strength, stability, sustenance, and peace.

—*Susan E. Ramsden*

No Gifts Please

You parents—if your children ask for a loaf of bread, do you give them a stone instead? Or if they ask for a fish, do you give them a snake? Of course not!
MATTHEW 7:9–11

As our extended family began to grow, choosing appropriate gifts for each other at Christmastime became more and more filled with tension. We wondered if the gifts we brought would be welcomed, and we dreaded opening our own packages because we usually either exchanged them or gave them to charity. Adding to our disillusionment was the fact that, by the time our nephews and nieces matured into their teens, they asked for money instead of gifts.

We thought of the scripture verse that told us to give our children "good gifts," not a "stone," and we decided money would not be a "good gift." Somewhere along the way, the whole Christmas scene had lost its meaning, and we needed to bring our celebration back to its original purpose and meaning. Would the rest of the family agree?

We had a family conference to discuss the whole idea of gift giving and to ask if there might there be a better way to celebrate this important holiday. Surprisingly, everyone, including the teens, agreed that there ought to be a more joyful and heartwarming way to celebrate the birth of our Savior. Out of that meeting came the decision to stop gift-giving altogether. We wanted warm memories, not gifts.

That was decades ago. Now, we get together for a sumptuous meal and read the Gospel stories of our Lord's birth. Our family takes time to reflect on the reason why we celebrate Christmas. We count our blessings and thank God, who loved the world so much that He came to Earth in human form so that everyone who believes in Him shall have eternal life.

My most treasured Christmas gift of all was, "No gifts please." Give me the memories anytime. If I need a toaster, I'll buy it myself.

Memories to treasure make the best gifts.

—*Evelyn Rhodes Smith*

January 3

The Christmas Sacrifice

*J*ust days before Christmas, I left my forest home to travel to a nearby city for materials to make gifts. Soft flakes of snow fell on my windshield as I passed along sparkling fields of white powder, but the wonder of it was lost on me. We had less than a hundred dollars to buy gifts for my parents, our five married children, and fourteen grandchildren.

On top of that, I had to buy the fixings for five people for Christmas dinner. The impossibility of it all overwhelmed me. I forced myself to hum along with radio carols, but it did little to lift my spirits. By the time I reached the outskirts of the city and bumper-to-bumper traffic, I wished I had stayed home.

Although red ribbons adorned doorways and strings of colored lights twinkled along storefronts, any Christmas kindness appeared to have vanished in the clamor of honking horns and shouting people. Everyone was in such a big hurry, and I couldn't figure out what the commotion was about. Couldn't people slow down long enough to enjoy the moment, listen to Christmas carols on the radio, or smile back at the waving Santa? If we couldn't have money, couldn't we at least have some goodwill?

The throngs of grumpy people made me think of how all but one of my five children would be unable to join us for this Christmas season. In addition, out of fourteen grandchildren, Rachel, would be the only one to celebrate with us. I feared she would be bored and lonely. At least my parents lived nearby, but my mother was due for a minor operation the day before Christmas Eve, and she wasn't sure she would feel up to company.

It was a relief to get out of my car and enter the craft store. It smelled of cinnamon-scented pine cones and vanilla candles. The frantic beat of my worried heart slowed, as I felt myself begin to relax.

The first person I noticed as I headed to the bead bins was a young man with sparkling, brown eyes. He reminded me of the hippies back in the sixties. His blond hair stuck out in all directions and spilled over his ears. I thought of a time years ago, when I had pulled my husband's hair into a ponytail and cut it off. I was on the phone calling a barber while he sat in the chair with tufts of cut hair clinging to his shirt. "It'll grow back," I had assured him.

This young man's hair had the distinctive look of a home cut, which immediately endeared him to me. "I'm Billy," he said. "I'm in charge of customer service, and I'd be delighted to help you."

He showed me how to spread mixed beads over felt-covered trays to make my job of finding the perfect ones easier. Then he went the extra mile by helping me in my search. We talked as we looked, and I was surprised to learn that he had two children and a wife to support. He looked younger than his years. He told me that this was his last day of work. He had found a job as a telemarketer for very little pay, but he was willing to do anything to provide for his family.

I told Billy about the loss of our home to fire when our children were young, a tragedy that forced my husband to take jobs picking onions and corn. Later, we passed out free laundry detergent door-to-door for a major company. I explained how I had to sling a thick leather strap over my shoulders and connect the ends to a heavy wooden tray in front of me. It was heaviest when it was full of the bottled liquid samples. "I threw some of those samples at angry dogs," I said. "It was my only protection, and a good way of lightening my load."

Billy threw his head back and laughed. One of those big throaty laughs that had me laughing along with him. My heart no longer felt heavy. The more we talked, the more I realized just how much God had done in our lives. We had a lot to be thankful for.

One by one, curious shoppers joined us at the bead bins until we had quite a crowd. Many of them shared their own stories of hard times and dwindling finances. Some told of how they made it through those times while others spoke of their fear of an uncertain future.

Most of the group were making their Christmas presents because they didn't have enough money for store-bought items.

"Homemade is better anyway," Billy said. "It's a gift from the heart."

"Just like the drummer boy did for Jesus," a small child said.

Billy smiled at him. "Yes. And just like Jesus did for us."

I looked at the faces bending over the bead trays. Not one showed any sign of being offended. At a time when "Happy Holidays" was quickly replacing "Merry Christmas," it was a joy and pleasure to discover that speaking the name of Jesus still invoked wonder.

Billy went on to tell of how he had recently cut eighteen inches of his hair and donated it to charity. We all stared at him in astonishment. "Why did you do it?" I asked.

He smiled and ran his fingers through his unruly curls. "I decided I had a better chance to get a good job if I cut my hair."

I felt myself choking up. Billy had sacrificed part of his identity for the love of his family. I stopped talking and said a silent prayer for God to open doors of opportunity for this young man. Chattering voices drifted around me, but I paid little attention to the words until I realized that one woman was in the process of hiring Billy to work on her computer. As it turned out, he had a degree in computer science, and several people took his business cards and promised to call. I praised God for His speedy answer to my prayer.

Jesus is the one who made the ultimate sacrifice for us. By leaving His glory in Heaven to become human, He left His God-identity behind. He was still God, but He looked like one of us. It was the first time I realized just how much our Savior had given up in leaving the magnificence of Heaven to reach out to us in love.

Billy and I shook hands and I left the store with renewed joy and a sense of wonder. Traffic was still heavy; drivers were still angry; but peace reigned in my heart. The Christmas season in which my husband and I couldn't afford to buy a single gift for one another turned out to be one of the richest. Perhaps we couldn't buy presents, but we could give each other the gift of our love and full attention. Perhaps my whole family couldn't be there, but the family that could was still very precious. I found myself getting excited about spending the time with them.

Who needed to buy gifts when the best gift of all—the gift of God's perfect Son—was perfectly free?

—*Sandy Cathcart*

The Cup of Love

And we know that God causes everything to work together
for the good of those who love God and are called according
to his purpose for them.
ROMANS 8:28

As a young couple, my husband and I had little, but on our first Christmas, we splurged. Since my dad suffered from allergies, I had never experienced a real Christmas tree, so my husband and I purchased a lovely, living pine tree to decorate for the holidays.

To the tree's dismay, I often forgot to add water to its little bowl. Soon, the needles fell like the brown and crispy leaves in fall. Tim consoled me. "It's like a plant, sweetie. It needs water to live—at least until Christmas."

Easier said than done, I thought.

Christmas arrived in normal fashion. I gave Tim a pair of shoes, and he surprised me with a miniature sailboat to add to my collection. A few days after the festivities, Tim took the dead pine tree "up the river" to be recycled.

Soon, the new semester began. One day, Tim, who had studied to be an educator in Industrial Technology, also known as a shop teacher, walked through the door with a small package. "Here," he said and handed me the gift. "I made this for you."

"What is it?" I tore apart the wrapping paper and discovered a wooden cup. "Where did you get this?" As I spoke, I turned the cup over. On the bottom, I read the words, "OUR FIRST CHRISTMAS TREE," followed by the date. Laughter and tears mingled as I gave him a hug. "I thought you recycled the tree?"

"I did," he replied, "but I cut off the stump first. After wood class, I stayed late a few times and turned it on the lathe." He took my hand and looked me in the eyes. "I figured you'd like a reminder of our first Christmas tree. Plus, you can't kill it."

I feigned indignation and gave him a gentle slug on the shoulder. Then I placed the wooden cup on the entry table for all our visitors to see. My cup made from love.

God can take our mess-ups, mishaps, and failings and "turn" them into beautiful works of His love. Simply trust Him with the pieces and know He has a perfect plan. Then, wait for Him to reveal His masterpiece. You may be surprised how He can use those dead tree moments to create something wonderful and lasting.

God's love is powerful enough to use even our most awful failures for His majestic glory.

—*L. A. Lindburgh*

January 4

The Case of the
Missing Gifts

"Where's Jon's camera?" I shouted. With Christmas music blaring in the background, my husband had just finished putting up the tree lights. It was obvious he didn't hear me the first time, so I repeated the words slowly and deliberately. "Where's Jon's camera?"

Still no answer.

I walked calmly over to the tree, placed my husband's face in my hands, and repeated the words, "Okay, Mark, where did you hide the Christmas gifts because I'm in no mood to play 'reindeer games.'"

Mark wrapped his arms tightly around my waist, planted a kiss on my cheek, and said, "C'mon, honey, where's your Christmas spirit?"

I wiggled out of his embrace and looked directly into his eyes. "Hand over the gifts and no one will get hurt. Understand?"

Mark chuckled. "I just love it when you get feisty like that."

It was December 19, 2007, and I felt rather smug about the fact that I had accomplished everything on my Christmas to-do list, except one thing—wrap the gifts. I thought my husband was trying to slow me down long enough so he could unravel the tangled web of Christmas tree lights and get them up before Jon arrived home from Grove City College in Pennsylvania.

"Okay, that's enough. What did you do with them?" I demanded.

Mark's look of surprise stunned me; he was telling the truth. After thirty years of marriage, I could tell the difference between a lie and a "half-truth." Mark's nostrils always flared when he was trying to hide something from me, but this time, those nostrils stayed put. He really didn't know.

A huge lump formed in my throat as I tried to sputter out the words, "The gifts are gone!" I finally blurted out.

Mark looked puzzled. "That's simply not possible. Maybe you misplaced them, sweetheart!"

"All of them?" I countered. "I don't think so!"

We searched the house: the basement, the attic, under the beds, inside the dryer, behind the washer, and in the car trunk, but we came up empty. No gifts. Back inside the house, I slumped down in the kitchen chair to reflect on what could have happened. Then, I remembered.

Two days before, I left the house for a few hours without locking the door, something I rarely did. I had a few writing deadlines to accomplish, so I headed for my favorite Internet café with free Wi-Fi. I enjoyed a bowl of cappuccino and a pumpkin spice muffin and promised myself I wouldn't leave the premises until the job was done.

A few hours stretched into six before I returned home. There was nothing misplaced, and the Christmas tree was still standing, so I assumed there was no harm done. What I had forgotten were the Christmas gifts lying in the middle of the basement floor, waiting to be wrapped. That's what I had missed until now.

"Honey, I think I know what happened," I said softly.

"What?"

I cleared my throat and made a full confession, "I left the door unlocked when I went out for a few hours a couple of days ago, but I didn't notice anything missing because the gifts were all in the basement."

I felt a tear trickle down my cheek as I watched Mark's face transform into total disbelief. "I guess I might have left the 'Pombo Department Store' open for business," I said.

"Are you saying that we've been robbed?" he asked.

I nodded my head sideways, then up and down.

There were five shopping days until Christmas, and that was definitely more days than money. We simply couldn't go out and buy new gifts for the family; it wasn't in our budget. One of the first purchases on my Christmas list had been Jon's camera. He put in the request a year in advance, and I couldn't wait to see his face on Christmas morning when he opened it. Now, there would be no camera—nothing. I called Jon first.

"Jon, I have some sad news!"

There was a long pause. "What is it, Mom?" he asked. "Did someone die?"

"Oh no, nothing like that," I said. Jon's inquiry set the stage for my second confession. The words trickled out, "We . . . I mean I . . . left the front door unlocked a couple of days ago."

"So what? You always do that."

Despite the newly formed lump in my throat, I continued my miserable tale. "Well, this time I left it open for someone else to take all of our Christmas gifts." I said through the newly formed lump in my throat.

There was another pause, this one longer than the first. "Jon, are you still there?"

I could tell by his silence that he understood the reality of my words. There would be no presents under the tree. My tears spilled into the phone receiver, onto the stack of Christmas cards, and seeped into the keys of my laptop.

"I'm so sorry, Jon. They even took your camera." Now, I'd done it. I spoiled the surprise, and then I told him he wouldn't be receiving the gift he most wanted. What kind of mother was I?

"Mom, it's okay. I mean that. Let's do what we used to do on Christmas."

"What's that?" I asked.

"Let's read the Christmas story."

I thought my ears had betrayed me, so I asked again, "I'm sorry, honey, I didn't hear you the first time. Did you say, 'read the Christmas story'?"

"Yeah, Mom, that's what we used to do. Remember?"

How was it that my son understood the true spirit of Christmas, while I had obviously forgotten? My heart was in my throat. Was he in a state of shock, or were all those years in "training" beginning to pay off?

There was a time in our lives when we didn't have money for gifts. We struggled to put food on the table and gas in the car, but those were the best Christmases. We made ornaments out of salt dough, drove downtown to see the lighting of the Christmas tree when we couldn't afford one of our own, and came home to read the nativity story from the *Big Book of Bible Stories* while we sipped hot cocoa with marshmallows.

I had almost forgotten how simple Christmas used to be. My eyes sparkled with fresh tears and a smile spread across my face. "Yes, Jon, I do remember, and I think that's a wonderful idea. I love you," I whispered.

Jon arrived home from college two days later. On Christmas morning, we awoke to a tree full of colored twinkling lights. It was decorated with simple dough ornaments and red velveteen bows just like the ones Jon had remembered. There were no presents, but we placed a gold star at the top of the tree to remind us of the Star of Bethlehem that guided the Wise Men to find the Christ child over two thousand years ago.

Afterward, Jon pulled out his worn, leather Bible from his backpack—the one we had given to him when he was six years old—and read the Christmas story from the book of Matthew. I reached over and grabbed Mark's hand as he brushed tears from his eyes.

That was the best "Pombo Family Christmas" we ever had. We rarely think about the presents missing under the tree, but we will always remember the true spirit of Christmas that filled our hearts.

—*Connie K. Pombo*

Through the Eyes of a Child

*But Jesus said, "Let the children come to me. Don't stop
them! For the Kingdom of Heaven belongs to those who are
like these children."*
MATTHEW 19:14

Christmas has seen a lot of phases at our house. Through
a toddler's eyes, the boxes and packaging proved much
more interesting than the contents. The preschool child
could hardly contain her excitement as she picked out
the biggest, tastiest cookies for Santa's plate and sprinkled reindeer food in the yard to guide the sleigh to the
right place. The teen set her sights on the latest and
greatest electronics. Each phase had its own magic, but
it was the eyes of my six-year-old daughter, Hannah, that
helped me focus on the greatest gift of all.

Hannah was particularly giddy about Christmas that
year. She led the production of decorating the tree, set up
the Nativity, taste-tested the cookies, and decorated her
own stocking. Although she didn't have money to buy
gifts, she was more than eager to give them. With great
enthusiasm, she dug through her toy bucket and her closet,
looking for little treasures to share. She dragged the paper
and bows into her room and proceeded to wrap dolls, cars,

and stuffed animals for us. She even placed fancy ribbons on each gift and labeled them in her careful six-year-old printing.

It was a real joy to watch our little elf in the Santa hat pass out her gifts and watch with eager anticipation as each one was opened and thanks expressed. The last gift Hannah gave us was a true surprise. We looked at the flat, seemingly empty piece of wrapping paper, folded up to look like a gift, and we couldn't help but laugh at her surprisingly mature sense of humor. Then she urged us to look closer. On the inside of the gift wrap, she had printed, "The gift of Jesus."

You are never too old to look at Christmas through the eyes of a child.

—*Becky Alban*

January 5

Why He Came

Some years are better than others. 2004 was one of those "others." It began as a normal year, but as the months ticked by, I realized it would go down in my history as a pretty rotten year. I had planned on launching a new business, but that door slammed shut when I found out in February that we were going to have a third child. Not that having a third child is bad, but when it catches you off guard, you're almost forty, and you're so ready to finally leave the "having babies" stage, it's not the best news. "God," I cried out one day in sheer frustration, "will I ever have time to do anything for myself?

Then, as the late spring snowmelt finally arrived in Colorado, my mother phoned from Ohio. "I decided to take you up on your offer to come visit for a while," she said. This announcement was both good and bad. My mom had been fighting ovarian cancer for two years and had decided against conventional treatments. I mentioned that Colorado had many alternative cancer facilities, and I suggested she should stay with us while she checked them out. My mom and I were always very close, and although I wanted to see her, I was anxious about stepping into a new role as her caregiver.

She stayed for three months. Then one day, she announced, "I think I need to go home and be with your father now." I sensed she had given up the fight. The past three months had been the most stressful I had ever endured. When we said our goodbyes, I couldn't help but wonder if I would ever see her again.

In my last trimester of pregnancy, my aches and pains provided a constant reminder that I considered myself too old to be having a baby. Finally, the big day arrived. On October 10, our "surprise" child was born, and in the process, threw us another curve ball. Throughout the pregnancy, we had been told my baby was a girl. So, when my midwife exclaimed, "She's a he!" the pink blankets and purple booties went back to the store. Good thing I never had time to decorate the nursery.

We scrambled to come up with a boy's name, and we decided on Chandler after learning it meant "light bearer." Later, I realized how appropriate our choice had been, as Chandler's presence shone a ray of light into an otherwise dark period of my life. As I gazed lovingly into his perfect, angelic face and marveled at God's handiwork, I was also saddened, knowing that he and my mother would probably never meet this side of heaven. My intuition became reality when my mom passed on December 15. I comforted myself with the thought that she would be in her Savior's arms on Christmas—her favorite holiday.

My husband and I flew to Ohio for the funeral and stayed a few days to help my dad in whatever way we could. My son, who stayed in Colorado with my mother-in-law, turned eight on December 21. For some reason, all the emotions of the previous months came crashing down on me like a tsunami wave when I thought of his birthday. I had always gone all out for my kids' birthdays, making them as special as possible. That year, I couldn't even be with him on this important day. Overwhelmed with heartache, I yelled at my husband, "I'm canceling Christmas this year."

"I don't think we can do that," my husband replied softly.

By December 23, we were home, and my older children would not let me forget about Christmas. They and Grandma had decorated the house while we were gone. The tree looked beautiful, with its lights twinkling and a bounty of presents perfectly arranged under its branches, but I still didn't feel like celebrating. Even Christmas morning, as I watched the kids open presents against a beautiful wintry backdrop of softly falling snow, I couldn't shake my "Bah, Humbug" spirit.

Hesitantly, my husband asked the family, "What do you say we go visit some of our friends in the senior center tonight?"

I wondered if he had gone crazy. The last thing I needed to do was spread my gloom to people who were trying their best to actually enjoy the holiday. "I don't think so," I replied quickly. "It probably wouldn't be a good idea for me to be there. Maybe you can just take the kids."

My husband was insistent. "No," he said, "this is just what you need. You know how much you love being with the people at the center. It'll do you good."

"It may do *me* good, but it certainly won't help *them* any," I replied. "Besides, we have nothing to bring them." Normally, we would have baked cookies or asked the kids to make Christmas cards. I had nothing prepared.

"That doesn't matter. They'd just love to have some company." As much as I hated to admit it, my husband was right. I didn't feel like going, but I decided it was better than sitting home.

When we arrived, my husband made the rounds with my oldest son and our newborn, while I visited residents with my four-year-old daughter. After stopping by several rooms and wishing everyone "Merry Christmas," my daughter and I turned down a long hallway. "If I remember right," I said to Cayla, "Miss June lives down this hall. It would be good to see her again."

We met June nearly five years ago. She didn't have any family, so I felt inclined to visit with her whenever possible. Each time we talked, I tried to share some aspect of the Gospel with her. She was raised in the church, but she had never given her heart to the Lord. Even so, she liked me to pray for her and read her the Bible.

I peered into what I thought was her room. She recognized me before I even saw her. "Well, Missy," she said cheerfully. "How've you been? I was hoping to see you for Christmas."

"Hi, June. How are you?" I asked in my best attempt to appear upbeat.

After a few moments of visiting, June leaned over and touched my hand. "I'm glad you came. I have a present for you."

"A present? Did you make me something?" Now, I felt terrible about not bringing gifts.

"Well, I didn't exactly *make* anything," she said. "My Christmas present is that I asked Jesus into my heart last week. I've really been thinking about all you've told me. I know I need God in my life. Since I'm not getting any younger, I guess it's now or never!" she exclaimed, and her eyes welled up with tears.

She and I cried. Then my daughter, who was looking at us as if we had lost our minds, decided to join in. Just then, the rest of my family came to June's door. My husband looked as if he might scold me for upsetting June, but I held up one hand. "It's not what you think," I said. "Wait until you hear the wonderful news!"

From that day, my entire perspective of Christmas changed. It's not about the things we have to give to others—it's about "who" we have to give. I lost so much in 2004 that I believed I had absolutely nothing to offer anyone. I wanted to avoid Christmas altogether, but even without gifts, joy, or even a good attitude, God had my back. He had already given me Jesus to share with June over the years, and He knew this was the year I would need her present the most.

Jesus came to seek and save *people* who are lost, but He also came to redeem those *things* that have been lost. When my mother died, our family lost a precious life, but we gained a new one with the birth of Chandler. I gave up my dream of starting a business, but God put me on His path of encouraging others through writing instead. I lost my peace and joy due to all the stress of the year, but God replaced those things and more when I received June's present.

At Christmas, we celebrate Jesus' birth, as well as all the wonderful people and blessings He's given us. During the chaos and distractions of the season, we shouldn't forget to give God's greatest gift to as many people as possible. God gave His Son to you and me and the Junes of the world, but He doesn't want *anyone* to miss out on His gift. That's why He came.

—Renee Gray-Wilburn

A Humble Package

There was nothing beautiful or majestic about his appearance,
nothing to attract us to him.
ISAIAH 53:2

When my kids were younger, I wrapped their gifts and set them under the Christmas tree. Even though I told them they had to wait until Christmas to open their presents, I would catch them shaking packages. Sometimes, they picked one up to smell it or listen to it. They would discuss amongst themselves what they thought the present was and even talked about what they would do with their anticipated gift. They always paid more attention to the largest packages.

The waiting was so hard! It seemed like Christmas would never come, but it always did. When it finally arrived, they ripped through the gifts looking for the best one, quickly casting the others to the side.

Since the beginning of human history, God told His people He would send a Messiah. Throughout the Old Testament, He sent prophets to let them know their gift was coming. Still, the time had to be right. Everyone talked about the coming of the Messiah—God's Son.

JANUARY 5

They speculated as to what He would look like. Everyone tried to figure out what He would do when He arrived.

After all the waiting, God sent His greatest gift in the most humble wrapping. He sent His Son to lie in a manger swaddled in a plain cloth. Who could possibly know that this gift truly contained all of heaven? The heavenly host of angels was moved to glorious awe when God brought Jesus Christ to Earth.

How often do we just take a quick look at Jesus and then toss Him to the side for a more spectacular package? Jesus is all we could ever want or need! Even when we cast Him to the side, He is the eternal gift that never leaves us or forsakes us. Father, help me to open my heart to receive even more of Jesus.

O come, let us adore the eternal gift that keeps on giving.

—*Eva Juliuson*

PART FOUR

EPIPHANY

INTRODUCTION

For many years, I used the word "epiphany" and knew that it meant a simple, yet striking realization, but it wasn't until my twenties that I discovered the connection with the birth of Christ. In Western Christian cultures, January 6 is celebrated as Epiphany. It commemorates the visit of the Wise Men to the Christ Child and their recognition of Him as Savior and King.

The Magi were wealthy, learned men who followed the patterns of the stars religiously. They had seen a strange, unknown star in the heavens, one that foretold the birth of a king. King Herod ordered them to follow the star and find the new king, so the Wise Men commenced their long and arduous journey. Even though most of us associate the Magi with the night Christ was born, most biblical scholars estimate that Jesus would have been between one and two years of age when the foreign travelers finally arrived.

The Bible doesn't identify the Wise Men by name or tell us how many there were, but it does state that they brought three gifts: gold, frankincense, and myrrh. Scripture also describes how God warned them not to return to

Herod as ordered because Herod, intimidated by the prospect of a new king, had made plans to kill the child.

Although January 6 is not regarded as an important holiday by many Christians in western culture, the churches that observe Epiphany believe that the experiences of the Wise Men contain some very important lessons for believers. Their long and devoted search for the Christ child, their worship and gifts, and their eagerness to share what they had found should remind us that there is more to Christmas than the birth of Jesus.

Christmas is a time for worship, praise, and gifts. Unless we follow the example of the Magi and spread the good news beyond the boundaries of our homes and churches, we are in danger of forgetting the real reason God sent His only Son as a gift of unconditional love.

January 6
Gracias, Hallelujah!

The difficulties began the day before Thanksgiving. One thing followed another until I began to question whether or not my family would have much of a Christmas celebration. Try as I might, I couldn't seem to muster up a festive spirit as the holiday season approached.

We prepared as well as we could for the extended family's Thanksgiving feast, but earlier in the month, my father was admitted to the hospital. Because we weren't sure when he would be released and how we could address his needs as well as prepare the meal, we ordered a turkey dinner from a local restaurant.

"It may not be quite the same," I explained to my son Keith, who would be flying in from California with his wife Suzan, "but we'll have the basics—turkey, dressing, cranberry sauce, and pumpkin pie. Aunt Donna has offered to fix the green bean casserole you like. Of course, we hope your grandpa will be home with us to celebrate."

Although Dad did come home the day before Thanksgiving, he had to return to the hospital Thanksgiving morning. In his weakened condition, he had come down with a debilitating stomach virus, one that subsequently ran through the entire family. My kids from California were sick along with the rest of us. Needless to say, it wasn't the fun visit we had all anticipated.

The virus passed, but only days later, I came down with a monster head cold that put me out of commission for several more days. Christmas was fast approaching. Would I put up any decorations? Would I be able to finish my shopping? Baking Christmas cookies was out of the question. There was also the matter of a previously planned trip to Mexico to visit my son-in-law's family. Would I be ready for that? I agonized over my father's condition and wondered if I should even go. I was physically and mentally challenged, and I struggled with how to manage everything. I felt conflicted and distracted.

"Father," I prayed, "I want so much to focus on the reason for the season, but I'm not doing very well here. Please help me center on you and truly celebrate the gift you gave us in the birth of your Son and our Savior all those many

301

years ago. I don't want to just endure the season, I want to rejoice in it and worship wholeheartedly. I trust you. Help me to know what to do."

Christmas Day came and went. We visited my dad once again, who was now in a nursing home for rehabilitation. It was a special time with the family, but somehow, Christmas just wasn't the same. Something was missing.

With Christmas behind us, my husband and I prepared for our trip to Mexico. We would travel with our daughter Melissa, her husband Rufino, and our seven-month-old granddaughter, Angelica, to be there over New Year's. It was Angelica's first trip to meet her paternal grandparents, aunts, uncles, and cousins fifteen hundred miles away.

We arrived in Mexico City without a hitch. I wasn't much of a world traveler, and I had only been to Mexico twice. Consequently, I had little experience with Mexico's culture and minimal communication skills, since I knew very little Spanish. Little did I know that a truly wondrous gift was waiting for me.

After a prolonged exit out of Mexico City's congested streets and a couple of additional hours on the road, we arrived in Ixmiquilpan, in northern Mexico. There, we found ourselves surrounded by warm greetings, gracious hospitality, and a family knee-deep in preparations for the next day's New Year's Eve celebration. Along with a guava dish and a fruit salad made with apples, the featured entrée would be chicken wrapped in cactus leaves and roasted in a stone-lined fire pit.

Rufino explained the Mexican tradition of "Las Posadas," a series of celebrations for nine consecutive nights, December 16 to 24, representing the nine months of Mary's pregnancy. Each night, the townspeople went to a different home for festivities, up until Christmas Eve, when they all gathered at the church for services. In Ixmiquilpan, the tradition of meeting in homes each evening continued through New Year's—and during our visit the celebration on New Year's Eve would be hosted by Rufino's family.

During the nighttime hours we not only feasted on good food and toasted each other, but we also participated in a candlelight procession in the street. Later, we laughed with the children as they gleefully tried to break the traditional candy-laden pinatas suspended above them over the street. It was great fun, and the group even coaxed me into the game where, blindfolded, I unsuccessfully attempted to smash the colorful clay-and-crepe-paper object. I laughed harder than I had in a long time.

The most memorable part of the evening was the celebration of the Christ child. Baby dolls that had been laid in the Nativity scene in the courtyard were swaddled reverently by the young people and carried throughout the group of people who had gathered. Christmas carols were sung, and sparklers illuminated the dark. As I looked around at the peaceful, worshiping faces around me, I finally felt the Christmas spirit. I was filled with awe and reverence as I rejoiced in the birth of the Son of man, God's gift to the world.

Joy and thanksgiving continued to buoy me in the following days. Before the trip was over, we would travel to Oaxaca, where another gift awaited me. We were in Oaxaca to visit Rufino's aunt, a nun in a convent there. Stepping into the convent's chapel, I stared in awe at the spectacular Nativity scene that was a focal point at the front of the room. It dawned on me how many Nativity scenes I had encountered throughout the trip, first in the family home, then in the city squares we had visited, and now in the chapel. Later I learned that *nacimientos* are Mexico's main Christmas decoration and many are kept on display until February.

In the chapel, music filled the air as a number of sisters began singing. At first, I was only aware of the fact that they sang in Spanish, and I couldn't understand them. Suddenly, their words rose and swelled, piercing the wall that had built up around my heart. "Gracias, hallelujah!" they sang. "Gracias, hallelujah!" Over and over the refrain rang out.

As I listened to the words and gazed on the Nativity, I realized what had been missing in the previous days. By concentrating on the stress and pressure of circumstances in my life, I had failed to walk with the one whose birth I was celebrating. In that illuminating moment I, too, could finally say, "Thank you, God! Praises to You!"

The day after our return home, I began unpacking, but I paused as I realized the significance of the date. It was January, 6, which in Mexico is known as Dia de los Reyes, or Three Kings Day. Mexican children eagerly await the gift-giving celebration that occurs on this special day which symbolizes the Wise Men bearing gifts for the baby Jesus. Once again, I marveled at everything I had heard and seen in Mexico's Christmas season, and I praised God for allowing me to be a part of it all.

—*Kenda Turner*

The Mysterious Magi

Jesus was born in Bethlehem in Judea, during the reign of King Herod. About that time some wise men from eastern lands arrived in Jerusalem, asking, "Where is the newborn king of the Jews? We saw his star as it rose, and we have come to worship him."

MATTHEW 2:1–2

It was a bitter cold night on Epiphany, January 6, in Kansas City. To celebrate the ending of the Christmas season, my pastor husband planned an outdoor worship service. The members of the church brought their used Christmas trees to the church parking lot. With permission from the fire department, we gathered around a huge bonfire and watched the trees being consumed.

The choir director led the congregation in singing carols. As we warmed ourselves around the burning trees, we heard distant voices singing the traditional Nativity hymn. "We three Kings of Orient are; bearing gifts we traverse afar."

Our eyes turned to the sound of the singing. Three shadowy figures came toward us, and we watched in awe while they trudged across the crusted snow on the field adjacent to the parking lot. As they drew closer, we saw three men dressed in royal robes. Taken by surprise, my husband asked innocently, "Who are you?"

"We are the Magi," the first king answered.

"Where did you come from?" the choir director asked, obviously bewildered.

"From the east," the third king responded.

Unable to contain his astonishment, my husband blurted, "Why are you here?"

The third king said, "We come bearing gifts." Then, in silence, the kings moved through the crowd and distributed chocolate candies wrapped in gold. Finally, as quietly and mysteriously as they had arrived, they departed another way.

As we watched the last fragments of Christmas trees turn to glowing embers, my husband thanked the choir director for his innovative addition to the Epiphany service.

"I didn't plan it," he said. "I thought you did."

Amazingly, no one present knew who was behind the unexpected visitors. The next day, my husband called the pastors of the surrounding churches. He wanted to thank them for their thoughtfulness by sending the kings to our worship service. Every pastor denied knowing anything about the incident.

The astonishing arrival of the Magi that evening forty years ago remains an unforgettable memory—and a mystery. When we recall the event, we smile at the memories of that strange occurrence. Our unlikely messengers reminded us once more of how God blesses us in remarkable ways. Nothing could be more astonishing and magnificent than the birth of Jesus Christ. That is the wonder and miracle of the Christmas season.

Live for the Lord and astonishing things will happen.

—*Barbara Brady*

CONTRIBUTORS

Gigi Adam has been a farmwife for fifty years. She and husband, Bill, have three sons and thirteen grandchildren.

Becky Alban lives in Minnesota with her wonderful, wacky family. She works with youth at church and school.

Monica A. Andermann is a writer living on Long Island. She is currently a member of Grace Lutheran Church located in her hometown.

Sandi L. Banks directs Summit Ministries' Adult Worldview conferences. She is the author of *Anchors of Hope* and a contributor to *Readers' Digest* and numerous other compilations.

Alma Barkman of Winnipeg, Manitoba, Canada, is a freelance writer and author of seven books. For more info visit her website at *www.almabarkman.com*.

Cindy Beck is an author, photographer, and dreamer. She lives in Utah with her husband, Russ, and their dog, Corky Porky Pie.

Edith Tyson Bell is a retired librarian and teacher. She has written book reviews, short articles, and since retirement, has published a book, *Orson Scott Card, Writer of the Terrible Choice* (as Edith S. Tyson).

Jamie Birr's publishing credit include *A Cup of Comfort*® *Devotional for Mothers* and *Centered on Love: Daily Devotions*. She lives in northern Indiana with her husband and three children.

Laura L. Bradford's writings appear in *Life Savors, A Cup of Comfort®*, and *Chicken Soup for the Soul* book compilations.

Barbara Brady lives with her husband, Merris, in Topeka, Kansas. They are blessed with three children and eight grandchildren.

Margaret Severson Brendemuehl cherishes her family and friends, and she loves working with flowers, food, and children.

Marcia E. Brown, a grandmother from Austin, Texas, has been writing family stories for fifteen years for magazines, newspapers, and anthologies including the *Cup of Comfort®* series.

Kay W. Camenisch and her husband, Robert, celebrated their fortieth anniversary in 2009. Each Christmas they still decorate with the wooden snowmen.

Connie Sturm Cameron is a speaker and the author of God's *Gentle Nudges*. Contact her at: *www.conniecameron .com* or *connie_cameron@sbcglobal.net*.

Jean Campion is the author of historical novels *Minta Forever* and *Return to Rockytop*. She is a regular contributor to *Cup of Comfort®* volumes and has been published in *Chicken Soup for the Soul*.

Sandy Cathcart is a freelance writer, photographer, and artist who writes about the Creator and everything wild. *www.sandycathcart.com*

Beth Lynn Clegg of Houston, Texas, is an active member of Memorial Drive Christian Church, Disciples of Christ.

Jessica Collins lives in Oshkosh, Wisconsin, with her husband and son. She works as a product copywriter by day.

Karna Converse is a freelance writer. She lives in Storm Lake, Iowa, with her husband and their three children.

Katherine Ryan Craddock writes professionally for many prominent Christian nonprofits. She lives with her husband and three children in Chantilly, Virginia.

Virginia Dawkins has been published in *A Cup of Comfort®️ Devotional*, *A Cup of Comfort®️ for Christians*, and *A Cup of Comfort®️ Book of Prayer*. Contact her at *jtdawk06@aol.com*.

Midge DeSart is the author of *Maintaining Balance in a Stress-Filled World*. She lives with her husband, Keith, in the Pacific Northwest.

Elsi Dodge is a single, retired teacher from Boulder, Colorado, who travels with her dog and cat in a thirty-foot RV. She blogs at *www.RVTourist.com/blog*.

Connie Hilton Dunn is married and lives in Kansas City. Her three grown children have flown the nest.

Darlene Franklin (*darlenefranklinwrites.blogspot.com*) is the author of seven books and novellas, as well as over a hundred articles and devotions.

Becky Fulcher lives in Monument, Colorado, with her husband, two children, and their dog.

Mary Gallagher is a reading specialist and writer who lives with her family in southern Ohio. She has been published in *A Cup of Comfort for Christians®*.

Renee Gray-Wilburn writes extensively for the children's and Christian marketplace from her Colorado home, which she shares with her husband and three young children.

Valerie Kay Gwin is a freelance writer from central Nebraska. She has been published in *A Cup of Comfort® for Grandparents* and *A Cup of Comfort® for Families Touched by Alzheimer's*.

Cathy C. Hall is a writer and humor columnist whose work appears in magazines, newspapers, webzines, and assorted anthologies.

Lauren Jensen lives with her husband and two children in northwest Iowa.

Jewell Johnson lives in Arizona with her husband, LeRoy. They have six children and nine grandchildren. Besides writing, Jewell enjoys walking, quilting, and reading.

Eva Juliuson is a wife, mom, mamaw, Christian writer, and grief counselor who encourages a deeper prayer life with the Lord!

Jean Kinsey's creative nonfiction is published in multiple *Chicken Soup* books, *Disciples World*, *Cup of Comfort®*, and other inspirational publications.

Laurie Klein's award-winning works, including the classic chorus, *I Love You, Lord*, appear in journals, anthologies, music resources, and recordings.

Mary Laufer lives in Forest Grove, Oregon. Her work has been published in newspapers, magazines, and anthologies.

L. A. Lindburg is a stay-at-home mother of two boys. She and her family reside near the Omaha, Nebraska, metro area. She participates in and teaches Bible studies for youth and adults.

Katie Lovette teaches film and television at a local college and is published in nonfiction. The Christmas Story Tree is still decorated every year.

Jeanette MacMillan is an English major who has taught writing and a minister's wife who has written youth programs. She resides in Indiana with her husband, near their children and grandchildren.

Laurie A. Perkins lives with husband Philip in Needham, Massachusetts. She has published two suspense novels and assorted stories.

Connie K. Pombo is an inspirational speaker, writer, and founder of Women's Mentoring Ministries in Mt. Joy, Pennsylvania. She enjoys spending time with her "grown" family. You can reach her at *www.conniepombo.com*.

Linda Blaine Powell is a retired elementary teacher who loves to read, travel, and garden. She has been married for forty-five years and has two daughters and four grandchildren.

Richelle Putnam is a musician, freelance writer/playwright, and creative writing instructor, but first and foremost, she is a wife, a mother of four, and a grandmother of five.

Susan E. Ramsden lives in California with her husband, Howard. They are the parents of Kimberly and grandparents of Olivia and Luke. Susan enjoys encouraging others through her writing.

Gabriel Ricard writes short fiction, poetry, film and stage scripts, novels, essays, and reviews for music, books, and film.

Susan Kneib Schank lives in Missouri with her husband and daughter. She is a member of Harmony Vineyard Church.

Kim Sheard is a professional dog walker and writer who lives in northern Virginia with her husband and dog.

Donna J. Shepherd has hundreds of articles and devotionals to her credit. Her children's books feature short, playful rhymes and humorous illustrations. Visit Donna at *www.donnajshepherd.com*.

Evelyn Rhodes Smith and her husband, Ted, reside in a retirement community in Charleston, West Virginia. She is a freelance writer who is active in The Bible Center Church.

Molly Smith is a Bible study teacher and jail chaplain. She works as a secretary for a radio ministry, and she and her husband, Karl, have three adult children.

Penny Smith enjoys a teaching and writing ministry. She is the author of *Gateway to Growth and Maturity*.

Gay Sorensen writes a monthly column for her church newsletter, and her stories, articles, and poems have appeared in many publications.

Donna Collins Tinsley is a wife, mother, and grandmother. She has been included in several compilations and is the author of *Somebody's Daughter*.

Kenda Turner lives and writes in Cincinnati, Ohio, where she also enjoys reading, knitting, and making more plans to travel.

Elisa Yager has contributed to several Cup of Comfort® publications and is currently very happily unemployed as she pursues "Certified Professional Coach" status. Feel free to leave her feedback at *proud2blefty@yahoo.com*.

SUBJECT INDEX

SCRIPTURE INDEX